CHATHAM HOUSE PAPERS

JAPAN'S FOREIGN POLICY

CHATHAM HOUSE PAPERS

General Series Editor: William Wallace
East Asia Programme Director: Peter Ferdinand

The Royal Institute of International Affairs, at Chatham House in London, has provided an impartial forum for discussion and debate on current international issues for some 70 years. Its resident research fellows, specialized information resources, and range of publications, conferences, and meetings span the fields of international politics, economics, and security. The Institute is independent of government.

Chatham House Papers are short monographs on current policy problems which have been commissioned by the RIIA. In preparing the papers, authors are advised by a study group of experts convened by the RIIA, and publication of a paper indicates that the Institute regards it as an authoritative contribution to the public debate. The Institute does not, however, hold opinions of its own; the views expressed in this publication are the responsibility of the author.

CHATHAM HOUSE PAPERS

JAPAN'S FOREIGN POLICY

Reinhard Drifte

The Royal Institute of International Affairs

Routledge

First published 1990
by Routledge
11 New Fetter Lane, London EC4P 4EE

Reprinted 1990

Reproduced from copy supplied by
Stephen Austin and Sons Ltd, Hertford,
and printed in Great Britain by
Billing and Sons Ltd, Worcester

British Library Cataloguing in Publication Data

Drifte, Reinhard
    Japan's Foreign Policy – (Chatham House papers : ISSN
    0143 – 5795)
    1. Japan. Foreign relations. Policies on government
    I. Title II. Series
    327.52

ISBN 0–415–03234–2

For Geneviève

CONTENTS

ACKNOWLEDGMENTS

I should like to thank the participants of the study group on Japan held at Chatham House in November 1988 for their valuable comments on the first draft of this paper. I also gratefully acknowledge the support of the Royal Institute of International Affairs, in enabling me to undertake a research trip to Japan in 1988. I have appreciated the assistance given by the staff of the Institute's Publications Department and East Asia Programme, and, in particular, I am indebted to Brian Bridges, the former head of the East Asia Programme, for his helpful suggestions and encouragement.

September 1989   R.D.

1
INTRODUCTION

Since the end of the Nakasone era in 1987 the world has been watching with bewilderment the changes in Japan's domestic political scenery. These changes were brought about by scandals involving practically every member of the cabinet, notably the Recruit Cosmos share-peddling scandal, but their political effect was greatly heightened by widespread popular dissatisfaction with a change in the tax system, increased opening of the Japanese market to foreign products (especially agricultural imports) and rising land prices. Foreign attention focused not only on the domestic upheavals, but also on the question of whether Japan's leadership would be able to continue to keep up with the fast-moving political and economic developments in and around Japan. This interest reflects both on Japan's stature in the international economy and on the many expectations of its role in maintaining the international system.

These expectations derive from Japan's continued economic development against a background of relative decline in US economic and military power. Japan has become the world's second largest exporter and, since the end of 1986, its largest creditor nation. In 1988 it overtook the United States as the largest provider of overseas development assistance (ODA). In many high-technology sectors it has gained a strong position in the world market. Japan's investment flows abroad have increased dramatically since the surge of the yen against the dollar, reaching a total of US$33,364

1

million during FY 1987 alone. For its leaders the issue in Japan's relationship with the outside world is how to have a foreign policy which is compatible with its economic performance, without having commensurate military power, but which at the same time meets the differing expectations of its Asian neighbours and major Western allies.

Whoever is the prime minister of Japan is faced with conflicting pressures and constraints emanating from geography, natural resources, history, culture, language, domestic policies, the economic base and the international environment, all of which determine the scope and speed of any political intervention in Japan's relationship with the outside world. These constraints can be examined in the light of certain basic interests in Japan's current foreign policy, which can be summarized under the five following points:

1. In an international environment which is still predominantly bipolar in security terms, Japan is politically, economically and militarily closely linked to the United States. The size of its economic and technological base, however, necessitates substantial relations with the rest of the world. Moreover, growing multipolarity, inter-dependence and the weakening of the US position of hegemony are forcing Japan to reassess Japanese-US relations.

2. Geographic contiguity to a militarily assertive Soviet Union and the alliance with the United States, as well as its own economic and technological strengths, are putting pressure on Japan to become once again a major military power. Although most Japanese prefer to continue making a largely non-military contribution to stability in the East Asian region, military links between Japan and the United States have become much closer, and are aimed increasingly at supplementing some US security roles in East Asia.

3. Japan's singular and successful pursuit of economic goals, and the relative decline of the United States, have given rise to conflicts with Japan's major economic partners over trade, investment and technology, as well as over increased expectations of Japanese burden-sharing. The political strains thus created on all sides have, however, only complicated the solution to these conflicts.

4. Although Japan is geographically and culturally part of Asia, its political and economic system, together with its trade imperatives and postwar circumstances, have drawn it closer to the group of advanced Western democracies outside this region. The distance between Japan and the rest of Asia is accentuated by the difficult legacy of Japan's past imperialistic policies in the region (a legacy revived by Emperor Hirohito's death in early 1989), and by differences in social and economic systems. However, the economic dynamism of the Asian-Pacific area and its growing economic interdependence, spurred now by Japanese investment and increasing import capacity, and the political modernization of many Asian countries, are again drawing Japan closer to its own region. So much so, indeed, that some observers are forecasting the emergence of a regional economic bloc dominated by Japan.

5. Although Japan's economic expansion and changes in the economic environment are increasingly integrating the country into global affairs, the outlook of most Japanese and their political leaders is still rather parochial and this is, in turn, reflected in the domestic political system. Moreover, the concern of the Japanese for the preservation of their unique national identity makes it difficult to accommodate various external demands for smoother integration into the world economy and greater burden-sharing. Nevertheless, the last decade has witnessed astonishing changes in the domestic environment which have affected Japan's relations with the outside world.

The rapidly changing environment – both domestic and international – has spurred within and outside Japan a debate about the country's position in world politics and what role it should play. Those in Japan who consider that a Japan pursuing predominantly economic goals and avoiding divisive or difficult foreign policy choices would make the best contribution to the international environment are no longer the leaders of the discussion about Japan's place in world politics. There is a broad consensus in Japan that the country should become internationally more active and shoulder broader responsibilities, but that its contribution should be non-military. There is a growing realization that Japan needs an

3

international environment which is politically stable and economically prosperous. Business is conscious of the fact that Japan has to transfer manufacturing and financial assets abroad in order to avoid international criticism and to develop traditional as well as new markets. Thus the debate in Japan is no longer about the necessity or otherwise of internationalizing but about what it means in concrete detail and how far it has to go. To what extent must Japan become similar to other advanced industrialized countries? Must it abandon its traditional distribution system and agriculture? Does it mean to accept foreign workers and refugees? What should be the guiding principles in the conduct of international affairs? How can Japan shape new principles to be agreed by all other major international players?

The aim of this study is to analyse the major lines of Japan's foreign policy during the 1980s against the background of three concepts – bilateralism, regionalism and globalism – and to assess the problems and prospects for the future. Bilateralism, regionalism and globalism are not established concepts in the discussion of Japanese foreign policy, but they are a convenient method of structuring the numerous and intricate interactions between Japan and the outside world. Bilateralism refers to Japan's relationship with the United States, which will receive special attention because of its central importance to Japan's foreign policy. Regionalism is a shorthand for relations with the East Asian environment from which Japan is in many respects separated but with which it is becoming increasingly involved. And globalism, of course, encompasses the whole question of the international impact of Japanese policies. An examination of Japan's foreign policy in the light of these three concepts will allow a better appreciation of the conflicting forces which shape the outcome of foreign policy-making in Japan.

Chapters 2 and 3 of this paper analyse the historical and institutional basis of Japan's international relations. How is Japan equipped psychologically and institutionally to cope with the changes presented briefly above? The pervasive nature of international relations means that foreign policy is no longer the preserve of the Foreign Ministry alone; as in other advanced industrial nations, many other ministries and agencies, as well as private organizations of various kinds, are now becoming involved. The Japanese have also been active in private transnational groups like the Trilateral Commission, which make important contributions to developing a consensus on solving global issues and have at the same time contributed to the better integration of Japan into the world community.

Chapters 4 and 5 deal with Japan's reactions to recent changes in the international environment through the introduction of the conceptual framework of 'Comprehensive Security', which was developed against a less benevolent strategic background. The main issue will be the relationship with the United States, centring on security affairs, and how it affects Japan's relations with its Asian environment, including the Soviet Union. The limitations on a stronger political link between Japan and Western Europe, particularly the lack of a security-orientated relationship, will also be assessed.

Chapters 6, 7 and 8 consider the expansion of Japan's economy, as well as the restructuring of its domestic base and the consequent repercussions on the direction of the country's foreign policy. By being asked to contribute more to the support of the global economic order, the Japanese are increasingly realizing the political clout bestowed on them by their economic strength and have started to wield it in their interaction with the industrialized and developing worlds. Changes in the economic environment such as the spectacular rise of the yen, the growth of the 'four little dragons' (South Korea, Taiwan, Hong Kong and Singapore) and rising protectionism in many markets have given new directions to Japan's regional emphasis. Economic developments have also increased the importance of Japan's second biggest market, the European Community (EC).

The final chapter assesses Japan's likely role in the 1990s as an increasingly important political and strategic, as well as economic, world power.

2

CHANGING PERCEPTIONS OF THE OUTSIDE WORLD

The postwar setting

For over four decades, Japan's foreign policy has been dominated by its relationship with the United States. Until the beginning of the 1970s Japan hardly deviated from the US line. This was the result of the US occupation from 1945–52 after Japan's defeat in the Pacific war, and the overwhelming economic and strategic superiority of the United States worldwide, particularly in East Asia. Under these circumstances, and given the frail and dependent nature of their country's economy, Japan's conservative politicians under Prime Minister Yoshida Shigeru accepted US leadership. The Peace Treaty of San Francisco, reached in 1951 with 48 Western-orientated countries, gave Japan back its sovereignty and helped to reintegrate the country into the world economy and international relations. The Japanese-US Security Treaty in the same year provided Japan with cost-effective security protection, in return for which the country had to provide the United States with military bases in Japan and to shoulder rearmament commitments of its own, tailored to US needs. Japan's conservative leaders had few difficulties in accepting the 'cold war world', as they had no sympathy with communism at home or abroad.

The war in Korea reinforced their concern about Soviet intentions in Asia (Japan's war with China in 1895 and with Russia in 1904–5 had started because of differences over Korea), and demonstrated the US commitment to Japan's security. In addition the war and ensuing US procurement orders helped Japan out of a serious business slump. However, the Japanese leaders were less willing to accept the ostracism of the People's Republic of China, demanded by the United States, which excluded diplomatic relations until 1972. As the cultural cradle of Japan, China could count on many sympathies amongst the Japanese public, and Yoshida himself considered that US policy did not take into account the incompatibility of China and communism as well as of China and the Soviet Union.

Moreover, there was from the first no unanimous support for US leadership and its consequences. This gave rise to two conflicting political streams, which epitomize the dichotomy of Japanese politics and continue to influence Japan's transition from an economic superpower to a more active world power.[1] On the one hand, there is what may be called the 'System of the Peace Constitution', because it was the 1947 Constitution which became the rallying point of all those who wanted a Japan without military forces and involvement in the struggles of the outside world. Under the Constitution Japan forever renounced the right to wage war and the right to maintain any sort of military force, and instead put its trust in the 'peace-loving peoples of the world'. The Constitution reflected the disarmament of Japan and the disillusionment of its people with the militarism of the past. On the other hand, however, there is the comprehensive Japanese-US alliance system embracing political, military, economic and cultural areas. The 1951 Security Treaty integrated Japan into the East Asian strategy of the United States, allowed US bases on Japanese soil even after the end of the Allied occupation, and readmitted Japan into the Western world while excluding its Chinese and Soviet neighbours. During the Korean war and the Vietnam war this security link aroused in many Japanese the fear of their country becoming embroiled in an Asian conflict. Each system seems to exclude the other, yet the former would not have existed without the comfort of knowing that the United States would care for Japan's external security.

The apparent inconsistencies and fluctuations in Japan's foreign and security policies are the result of the need to balance both systems and construct bridges between them. There can be no doubt that the decision of Japan's political leadership to concentrate on the economy proved the most crucial factor in maintaining that balance. In the period immediately following the devastation of the Pacific war, this decision seemed only natural. Moreover, part of the original initiative for this strategy came from the United States, which encouraged the Japanese economy in order both to try to reduce the burden on itself and to contribute to regional economic development. In 1947 the United States launched the idea of Japan becoming the workshop of Asia (West Germany was mentioned as the workshop for Europe), in order to eradicate the poverty which was such fertile ground for the expansion of communism.

Japan's postwar leaders also realized that without a strong economic base there could be no political power. The first diplomatic White Paper in 1957 concluded that the only way to raise living standards and to increase national power lay in the peaceful development of economic strength. However, what may have been conceived by these leaders as a temporary policy gained a momentum of its own. As a result the economic effort took precedence over military power, and foreign policy became equated with foreign *economic* policy. Consequently, the Japanese continued, under the benevolent eyes of their US protectors and promoters, to concentrate on the economy even after reconstruction had ended. There was a short period of intense struggle in 1960 over the revision of the Security Treaty. This provided Japan with a more equal military relationship, to the satisfaction of most Japanese, but was vehemently though unsuccessfully opposed by the adherents of the Peace Constitution system. Then the new Prime Minister, Ikedo Hayato, proclaimed his famous '10-year income-doubling plan' – a target which was actually attained much faster, thanks to a booming world economy.

During the 1960s Japan also gradually relaxed its foreign-exchange regulations to permit Japanese foreign investment. This investment went overwhelmingly to Asia; particularly helpful were reparation agreements with several Asian nations, which prepared the way for entry into these markets. Under strong guidance from the United States, Japan and South Korea managed in 1965 to overcome domestic opposition and normalized diplomatic relations. In 1964 Japan was admitted into the Organization for Economic Cooperation and Development (OECD). It was an acknowledgment of Japan's growing economic power – sixth in the world in terms of Gross National Product (GNP). This move, together with the holding of the Olympic Games in Tokyo in the same year, contributed significantly to the Japanese perception of finally belonging again to the better part of the world community. In terms of total GNP Japan overtook Italy in 1966, Britain in 1967, France in 1968 and finally West Germany in 1969.

Domestic and American obstacles notwithstanding, the Japanese succeeded in building up a presence in the Chinese market once more. Whereas the Japanese tried to circumvent the political obstacles by insisting on the separation of politics from economics, the Chinese understood very well how to use Japan's economic interests in order to extract some political concessions. However, trade was subject to abrupt changes in China's economic and foreign policies, which rather limited the overall economic relationship until 1972.

The oil crisis of 1973 had a most profound effect on Japan's high growth rates and on its relationship with the outside world. It hit Japan where it felt most vulnerable: its dependence on oil as the key raw material for the economy. Because the major US oil companies decided to give priority to their domestic customers, Japan felt abandoned by its US ally. This feeling was aggravated by the so-called 'soya bean shock' – when US traders of soya beans suddenly threatened to reduce their supply to Japan because of a temporary shortage. The relative decline of US economic power was symbolized by the abandonment in 1973 of the fixed exchange-rate system established at Bretton Woods at the end of World War II. It became obvious that the United States was no longer able or willing to shoulder to the same extent as before the responsibility for the maintenance of the economic order which had been so beneficial to Japan. As a result the Japanese lost their hitherto unshaken confidence in the reliability of the United States as a partner.

9

The situation was not helped by an unending series of trade conflicts with the US, which began at the end of the 1960s with a dispute about Japan's textile exports. This was followed by disputes about Japanese steel and automobile exports and was accompanied by an increasing Japanese trade surplus with the US and later also with the European Community.

At the same time changes in the US security policies which affected Asia made many Japanese doubt the US security guarantee and subsequently start to question the wisdom of concentrating solely on economic matters. The US war in Indochina was criticized by most Japanese because they thought that the United States was using the wrong means for what they themselves considered to be basically a problem of underdevelopment and an aspiration for national unity. However, when the United States finally left Indochina and substantially curtailed its military presence in East Asia, the basis of Japan's pacifism seemed endangered and there was concern about the country being left alone in a sea of hostile currents. This feeling was strengthened by the withdrawal of one US army division from South Korea during the Nixon administration as part of the 'Nixon doctrine', which required a greater contribution for security matters from US protegés, and then the announcement, during the Carter administration, of a planned withdrawal of all US ground troops from South Korea, which was openly and strongly opposed by the Japanese government. It took most Japanese observers of US foreign and security policy in Asia some time to understand that the fundamental issue for US policy-makers was not how to withdraw from the region, but how to stay.

Although the establishment of diplomatic relations between the United States and the People's Republic of China in 1972 was widely welcomed in Japan, the 'abandonment' of a staunch ally like Taiwan, situated in Japan's immediate neighbourhood and along one of Japan's major sea lanes of communications, was regarded with a degree of ambivalence. The secretiveness of the US decision to normalize relations with China deepened Japan's disillusionment with the United States, for Japan's diplomatic representatives were still supporting the US Taiwan policy in the United Nations General

Assembly while Henry Kissinger was privately negotiating with China's leaders in Beijing.

Although the United States began to appear to the Japanese as a less reliable guarantor of their economic and security interests, the Soviet Union continued to build up its military forces in East Asia in the second half of the 1970s. The Japanese were particularly troubled by the increase of Soviet forces to a whole division on the so-called Northern Territories (i.e. the islands of Habomai, Shikotan, Kunashiri and Etorofu, off Hokkaido), which have been occupied by the Soviet Union since the end of the Pacific war and are still claimed by Japan. The Soviet support of the Vietnamese aggression against Kampuchea and Laos, and, more importantly, the Soviet invasion of Afghanistan in December 1979 (and the strong American reaction to it) signalled to Japan that the period of detente was over. The invasion of Afghanistan prompted the doveish Prime Minister Suzuki Zenko to speak for the first time of the potential Soviet threat. After the first oil shock of 1973–4 Japanese business had been interested in diversifying Japan's sources for raw materials and oil; this had increased interest in the Soviet Union. However, the end of detente also cut short expectations of acquiring Siberian raw materials at a price that was both politically and economically acceptable.

Changing perceptions of the outside world

Geography and population size are not only major factors determining the power of a country; they also influence its perceptions of the outside. Japan is a crowded archipelago at the rim of the Pacific Ocean, consisting of four main islands with a total area of 377,000 square kilometres, about the size of Finland, and occupied by 122 million people, of whom one third live in an urbanized belt stretching from Kobe to Tokyo along the Pacific coast. The lack of equally advanced neighbours prevented close horizontal economic or political integration with other Asian states in the first three postwar decades. However, progress in communications and transport, the shift of global economic dynamism to the Pacific, the advances of democratic movements in the region, the military and even

11

economic expansion of the Soviet Union in the Far East, and a modernizing China are now affecting Japan's geographic, economic and political isolation. These changes in the international environment clash with perceptions and behaviour which owe more to the past than to the present.

As a consequence of their country's long isolation in geographical and historical terms, the Japanese have developed a strong sense of uniqueness, of belonging only to Japan and of being different from other people, while eagerly seeking strength by absorbing elements from more advanced cultures, first from China and then from the West. The long historical experience of peace and the disaster of the militarist interlude this century have contributed to a low level of external threat perception and to pacifism. The feeling of isolation is enhanced by other factors. International communication is hampered by different methods of expression. The problem is compounded by poor foreign language skills, attributable to the structure of language teaching and the difficulty of the Japanese language for foreigners. These factors put certain limits on the development of relationships with the outside world.

Historically developed perceptions and behavioural idiosyncracies tend to linger on, while external circumstances are changing and new perceptions and behaviour modes are in fact coexisting with the old. The outside world has become more tangible than ever for the average Japanese through foreign products, exposure to foreign news and foreign travel.

An increasing number of Japanese come into contact with foreign products and foreign culture even without leaving their country. It is, however, open to question how representative these foreign products are, and how accessible they are for Japanese living outside the major cities or those with less money available to spend on usually overpriced foreign goods.

The Japanese media have extensive overseas reporting networks, while the foreign media are beginning to exploit the market potential by publishing in Japan. Also impressive was the launching in 1987 of satellite programmes by NHK, the Japanese national broadcasting network, featuring the most popular news broadcasts from the BBC, from ABC in the United States, and from Beijing, Seoul and

Bangkok. Although satellite receivers are not yet widespread, these broadcasts have a positive effect in bringing both Asia and the West closer to Japan. The Japanese in general thus have the opportunity, at least, to be better informed about the world than people in most other advanced countries.

The number of Japanese travelling abroad and staying overseas for an extended period is dramatically increasing. In 1988 8.4 million Japanese travelled abroad, an increase of 23% over the previous year. The appreciation of the yen is pushing these figures even higher. By international comparison, however, the percentage of Japanese travelling abroad is very low, at 4% of the entire population, compared to 39% in the United Kingdom, 34% in West Germany and 12% in the United States. The Transport Ministry is therefore aiming through various measures to increase the Japanese rate by 1991 to about 10%, the current percentage for Australia. Of the travellers in 1987, 34% went to the United States and 36% to Asian destinations. In the same year just over 500,000 Japanese were living abroad for an extended period. Over 10,000 Japanese schoolchildren are now returning annually from abroad; the numbers are increasing because of the rising number of employees of companies investing abroad and the cheaper education in other countries. While foreign visitors to Japan totalled only 2.1 million in 1987, showing a decrease over 1985 because of the rising yen, the number of foreign residents is increasing, particularly through the influx of cheap Asian labour, which is creating a new problem for Japan.

These developments have not failed to produce conflicting attitudes and perceptions of the outside world. The Japanese now better understand international interdependence and their growing integration into the world in general. In addition, opinion leaders created a cult of vulnerability for the Japanese nation, which was strengthened by the experience of the oil crisis. At the same time, however, there is a growing resistance to outside influences and pressures as well as concern about the effect of these foreign influences on Japanese society. Although the number of long-term Japanese residents overseas is increasing, it is still very difficult for Japanese to stay abroad for long periods because of the pressures to conform and the need to return in order to have a Japanese education and career pattern. Consequently, Japan has problems in filling its staff quotas in international organizations and finding qualified staff for technical cooperation in the Third World. Companies now often find it difficult to send their young employees abroad for a prolonged period because they do not want to expose themselves to the discomfort of an alien environment. There is also an ambivalent attitude towards schoolchildren returning from abroad, their foreign experience being seen not so much as an asset for Japanese society, but rather as something to be contained or eliminated. This attitude, however, is changing with the economy's growing need to interact more easily with the outside world.

The Japanese realize that foreign pressure, particularly from the United States, is increasing constantly and they often consider their leaders to be too compliant. The country's greater integration into the world in general and accompanying pressures to become more like other countries are also perceived as a loss of self-determination and sovereignty. Moreover, Japan's late arrival on the world stage meant that it was difficult to put a Japanese imprint on an international system which had already been basically shaped. Economic success has, nevertheless, bred a new self-confidence, especially amongst the younger generation, which has not experienced war and the hard years of economic rehabilitation, and which wants to be more assertive towards the outside world.

One manifestation of this rethinking is an intense preoccupation with what it means to be Japanese, the so-called *Nihonjinron*. Japanese culture, behaviour and thinking, it is argued, are unique and distinct from the rest of the world. So, on the one hand, the slogan of 'internationalization' enjoys great popularity as it is somehow vaguely perceived as being helpful both in filling the vacuum created by having surpassed all other models and in obtaining greater recognition abroad. On the other hand, this same 'internationalization' is seen as a danger to Japan's 'Japaneseness', which some conservatives want to fight for by the promotion of nationalism.

Paradoxically, therefore, the outside world's perception of Japan's homogeneity and cultural cohesiveness seems to be in inverse proportion to what the Japanese themselves feel about it. In reality, the Japanese suffer at the same time from an inferiority complex and a superiority complex. This is particularly evident in the Japanese attitude to their Asian neighbours, notably China, which is, on the one hand, admired as the cradle of Japanese civilization but, on the other hand, despised for its perceived failure to cope with modernization. This dual complex is compounded by an acute sense of hierarchy, epitomized by the vertical structure of Japanese society, in which age, status, position and so on are all significant. It is natural for the Japanese to tend to apply this approach also to international society. This affects their perception not only of developing countries, but also of developed countries, which Japan has now surpassed in terms of GNP and technological development. For example, for most of the 1980s the countries of Western Europe have been popularly perceived in Japan as not doing too well either in readjusting their economies to the challenges of the era of high technology or in running their social welfare systems. They were slipping steadily down the hierarchical ladder until the single European market process challenged this perception. One can assume, however, that as Japan gains experience of being a front runner in economic and political terms, a better understanding of international interdependence will balance this hierarchical view of the outside world.

3

FOREIGN POLICY ACTORS

Since 1948 Japan has been ruled uninterruptedly by conservative parties, and, since 1955, by the Liberal Democratic Party (LDP), which has really functioned as a coalition of factions. This has provided Japanese politics with a continuity which is very unusual among Western democracies. The political system has been explained as a triad of the ruling LDP, big business and the bureaucracy, but it has become considerably more diffuse in recent years. Until the 1970s foreign policy-making concerned with 'low' political content was left to the bureaucracy, which meant in practice the Foreign Ministry. During the 1980s the domestic political system has become more pluralistic, with a greater variety of groups gaining influence. The composition of the groups varies according to the nature of the issue at stake, but the system still revolves around the triad. This has also been true of foreign policy-making, which has always involved fewer actors than any domestic issue. The strong position of the bureaucracy is also enhanced by the fact that the prime ministers and cabinet ministers change more frequently than in other democratic countries. With the exception of Nakasone, no prime minister since 1972 has stayed in office for more than two years. Cabinet ministers, such as the foreign minister, rarely last for much more than a year.

The prime minister and the political parties

In spite of the constraints derived from the need to provide factional balance in the LDP, the prime minister is of central importance to the foreign policy-making process because of his function as the president of the ruling party and his constitutional position as the chief executive of the government. The latter function has been enhanced in recent years through the strengthening of the Secretariat to the Cabinet (*Naikaku Kambo*). Prime Minister Nakasone improved the crisis management and coordination functions of the Cabinet Secretariat when he reorganized its four sections in 1986.

More important, however, was the long incumbency of Nakasone himself, from 1982 to 1987, and his willingness to actively shape foreign policies through personal diplomacy, the use of personal emissaries and the establishment of unofficial advisory commissions with hand-picked members. The use of *ad hoc* commissions was started by Prime Minister Ohira Masayoshi in 1979, but Nakasone made particular use of them to try to overcome party or bureaucratic resistance. Advisory commissions related to external policies were created on defence policy (though its conclusions on abolishing the 1% ceiling on defence spending were not at first accepted by the LDP) and on international economic problems (leading to the Maekawa report on restructuring the economy). The improvement of relations with South Korea from 1983 was made possible through active diplomacy at summit meetings, the direct links between Nakasone and President Chun Do Hwan, and the use of Nakasone's personal emissary, Sejima Ryuzo. The most famous example of personal diplomacy was the so-called Ron-Yasu link between Nakasone and US President Ronald Reagan.

Prime Minister Takeshita was more interested in the party and was very efficient at getting the LDP behind him in order to carry out domestic policy change. To compensate for his previous lack of international exposure, he undertook frequent visits abroad. Moreover, his 'team player' spirit did not prevent him from pursuing an active personal diplomacy; for example, he impressed

17

the Western economic summit leaders in Toronto in 1988 with his forceful initiatives on developing country debt problems and his championship of the Newly Industrializing Economies (NIEs). Most Japanese parties are characterized by factionalism. Matters relating to the parity among factions have more importance than the ideological merits or flaws in a given foreign policy issue. The longevity of the LDP in power is due to its 'pork-barrel' approach to politics, although this has now become a threat to the unique position of the party in Japanese politics. Within the LDP the role of politicians in foreign policy has been hampered by a lack of experience and knowledge about international issues. Few diplomats start a second career in politics, compared with other bureaucrats from the Finance Ministry or the Ministry of International Trade and Industry (MITI). Nor has prominence in the field of international relations been considered as relevant to a successful political career. Nevertheless, in an age of growing international interdependence and interactions, this attitude has begun to change. Pictures in a Diet member's office showing him shaking hands with a foreign dignitary are now an asset. Traditional domestic concerns such as agriculture and fisheries have become key issues in bilateral and multilateral relations. As a result the number of Diet members participating in foreign policy-related meetings of the LDP has increased.

Many foreign policy issues are now discussed within the relevant intraparty committee (*bukai*). The main body for discussion on international affairs in the LDP is the Political Affairs Research Council, followed by the International Affairs Division. Another method of involving party members in foreign policy is the bilateral friendship organizations formed by Dietmen of the various parties. These organizations allow the LDP to maintain contacts with countries or bodies with which formal diplomatic relations do not exist, such as Vietnam, Kampuchea, North Korea and the Palestine Liberation Organization (PLO). Before the normalization of diplomatic relations with China in 1972, such groups were for a time responsible for concluding trade agreements with Beijing. In sum, foreign affairs now receive more attention from LDP politicians than ever before. Intraparty disputes, however, are now based more on conflicting material interests than on diverging ideological positions.

Finally, individual opposition parties have also been active in developing contacts with countries which are not officially recognized, such as the Japan Socialist Party's exchanges with North Korea. Otherwise the opposition parties, at least until now, have played hardly any role in foreign policy-making and have confined their foreign policy-related activities to the Diet. The defeat of the LDP during the elections for the Upper House in July 1989 has, however, increased the appeal of the opposition parties, and particularly the Japan Socialist Party, to the public, and they may be able to translate this into greater influence on foreign policy in future. At present, they can exert pressure on the government by asking embarrassing questions or by manipulating Diet procedures to make a point on problems of foreign policy and national security. These are topics on which they feel less constrained than, for example, on agricultural issues, over which they have to take into account the interests of their constituents. Owing to the dichotomy between Japan's foreign and security policies, defence issues are the subject of much popular attention. The government is particularly vulnerable each spring, when any delay in Diet deliberations can prevent the passing of the budget in time for the new fiscal year starting in April.

Big business

As in purely domestic economic issues, the leaders of the major economic organizations can exercise considerable influence on foreign policy-making. They are in particular the four main business associations – Keidanren (Federation of Economic Organizations), Nisho (Japan Chamber of Commerce and Industry), Keizai Doyukai (Japan Committee for Economic Development), and Nikkeiren (Federation of Employers' Organization). However, their influence tends to be overestimated abroad and there are no cases where one single business organization, such as the Keidanren, can actually speak for the whole of Japan's business or industry. The interests of business, industry and finance enter the decision-making

19

process through innumerable consultation bodies attached to the various ministries, in which representatives of the economic organizations meet those from government and the bureaucracy. The major economic organizations themselves have committees dealing with foreign policy issues, where policy recommendations for the government and the bureaucracy are worked out. Top businessmen on semi-official missions often travel abroad to conduct private economic diplomacy, reporting their results and impressions to the government. A Keidanren mission which visited several European countries at the end of 1981, for example, was instrumental in prompting the government (or at least making it politically feasible) to allow more compromises on trade matters.

Big business is, however, no monolithic block. Although Japanese industry often gives the impression to the outsider of being 'Japan Inc.', companies compete ferociously with one another within Japan, and this is something that adds to their strength vis-à-vis foreign companies. But it can also be a disadvantage; the intensity of the pluralism and the diversity of interests among Japanese companies prevented an effective common initiative in the trading relationship with China before 1972, allowing China to skilfully play one industry off against another.

Even now no consensus has been reached on the economic dimensions of Japan's security policy, as the question of business participation under the Strategic Defence Initiative (SDI) agreement with the United States, made in 1987, has shown. However, there is a growing number of high technology-related companies which would like to work more closely with the United States and particularly to abrogate the existing ban on arms exports. The Keidanren has been very positive on the liberalization of agricultural imports, because of a concern about the impact of an intransigent Japanese attitude on overseas markets for industrial products, and it has become, in effect, the most powerful domestic lobby for a wider opening of the Japanese market to foreign companies. The LDP's very factionalism, however, makes it difficult for any other body to exert effective influence, although the ruling party's rising financial needs make it increasingly dependent on contributions from companies as well as funds raised by economic organizations. However, the Ministry of

Finance, through its prerogatives, can regulate the speed of the opening-up of Japan's financial markets.

Apart from through business organizations, commercial interests are promoted abroad through various other means. In Washington, Japan has 133 registered lobbyists with an estimated annual budget of $60 million, the most powerful lobbying effort by any foreign country in the United States. As will be discussed below, sponsorship of Japanese cultural events abroad is growing with the increase in Japanese foreign direct investment (FDI).

In sum, the elaborate consultation mechanism between the business world on the one hand and government and the bureaucracy on the other ensures that economic interests enter the foreign policy decision-making process at all levels, while business organizations or particular economic interests also independently promote their line with foreign actors. As both the bureaucracy and the LDP are deeply committed to smoothing the country's economic advance abroad and as there is no major goal apart from preventing damage to the overall framework in which Japan wishes to operate as an economic superpower, the role of the government is to coordinate conflicting domestic economic interests, and to protect the greater national interest from particular economic interests.

The Foreign Ministry and the emergence of new actors

Within the bureaucracy dealing with foreign policy, the Ministry of Foreign Affairs occupies a central coordinating role. This role is no longer as undisputed as it was during the first two postwar decades. During the American occupation the Ministry considerably increased its political role, because, while many politicians were purged, the bureaucracy through which the Americans ruled Japan was largely left untouched and many bureaucrats entered the political arena. Two of Japan's most prominent prime ministers, Ashida Hitoshi and Yoshida Shigeru, were former diplomats. Moreover, bureaucrats from the Foreign Ministry had greater linguistic skills, which enabled them to communicate with the occupation forces. Finally, Yoshida's policy of giving primacy to the bilateral relationship with the United States became nowhere more entrenched than in the Foreign Ministry. All external issues were subordinated to the welfare of the Japanese-US relationship. Since the military relationship was at its very core, the division for security became part of the North America Bureau. As a result Japan's defence policy is still predominantly shaped and represented by the Ministry of Foreign Affairs, while the Defence Agency is responsible for operational aspects.

In comparative international terms, the Foreign Ministry's budget and personnel strength rank low. The budget of the US Department of State is 4.5 times as big as that of the Japanese Foreign Ministry, West Germany's is 1.9 times and Britain's 1.5 times bigger (1985 figures). Whereas other ministries have large funds for research and other purposes, the Ministry of Foreign Affairs has only the ODA budget to administer, although this is expanding fast. In terms of personnel the Ministry is understaffed, with only 4,060 officials in 1987, compared to 5,967 diplomats in West Germany (1984) and 6,498 (including staff of the home civil service numbering 1,882, as of 1986) in Britain. The annual intake of officials for the higher civil service is around 28, and 38 for the lower civil service.

By definition, the Ministry of Foreign Affairs lacks the domestic power base which most other ministries have in order to push their interests. However, it is on most foreign policy issues the sole coordinator and 'unifier' (*ichigenka*) of conflicting interests, a role which, in addition to its specialized knowledge about other countries, places it in a unique and strong position vis-à-vis other ministries.

The Foreign Ministry's greatest traditional rival in foreign economic policy is MITI, whose role has grown with the increased number of foreign trade issues which go to the heart of the Foreign Ministry's concern, i.e. Japanese-US relations. One major battle was over the opening of Japan's internal market to foreign products, which was finally decided at the beginning of the 1980s. MITI is now generally in favour of liberalization, and it is the Ministry of Agriculture which currently appears the most protectionist. However, there are several sectoral issues where the Foreign Ministry and MITI still clash, especially over high technology. A major power struggle developed over the COCOM regulation issue in 1987–8, when the Ministry wanted review power over the export of sensitive goods to socialist bloc countries. This arose out of a long-standing dispute over responsibility on matters relating to security, which the Foreign Ministry sees as its field of expertise (it does not, for example, acknowledge any special role for the Office of Security Trade – *anzen hosho boeki kanri shitsu* – in MITI, which is responsible for the implementation of the COCOM regulations).

Because of the increase in transnational relations, many more ministries have become involved in foreign policy matters and the Foreign Ministry has to rely on their expertise in fields ranging from AIDS to VAN (Value Added Networks). A growing number of bureaucrats from other ministries are on secondment either in the Ministry in Tokyo or its embassies. In 1987 there were 712 staff in the Foreign Ministry or its embassies on loan from other ministries, including 40 from the Defence Agency and the Self-Defence Forces (SDF). There were 53 diplomats on secondment to other ministries and agencies.

With the increasing number of 'low politics' issues demanding public support and understanding, the Foreign Ministry is trying to reach out and promote a better understanding of foreign policy issues within Japan. This has been described by the Ministry as Japan's 'internationalization from within' (*uchi naru kokusaika*). Diplomats are sent throughout the country to explain the fast changes in Japan's external environment to a wide public. With the growing contacts between ordinary citizens and the outside world, more assistance is needed. One indicator of such growing links is the existence now of 538 Japanese towns/regions with sister city links in 40 different countries. To foster such contacts the Ministry created the Consultation Centre for Internationalization (*kokusaika sodan senta*) in 1986. In 1988 it announced plans to create a new section to deal with resident and visiting foreigners.

The increase of transnational activities has also given rise to a greater Japanese participation in private and non-official international organizations, which have a beneficial effect in trying to bring people of various nationalities together, as well as helping the Japanese to understand the concerns of non-Japanese. For example, there are close to 200 non-governmental organizations (NGOs) concerned with development issues in Japan. An increasing number of Japanese are speaking up and making positive contributions at meetings of organizations such as the Trilateral Commission or the Bilderberg Conference. As more Japanese, especially younger people, master foreign languages, numerical as well as generational change is taking place in such participation.

Cultural diplomacy

Cultural diplomacy, too, needs to be seen as a major and increasing influence in Japan's transnational activities. The United States and the European powers put great emphasis on acquainting other peoples with their culture, civilization, way of life and language; the long history of European cultural influence has set certain standards which make it even more difficult for a latecomer to exert cultural influence. Until recently, Japan has had no cultural mission to compare with France, West Germany, Britain or the United States. Whereas the United States and France each spend the equivalent of over ¥100 billion on cultural exchange, Britain and West Germany ¥80 billion and ¥50 billion respectively, Japan's expenditure has reached only ¥18.5 billion.[2]

This negligence of cultural diplomacy is slowly changing. First, the government came to recognize that such activities as the organization of cultural events and Japanese language teaching could help to change Japan's image as an 'economic animal' and soften the bad impressions created by Japan's export expansion. Second, the recent increase in self-confidence and rising nationalism have provided the Japanese with the will to show off their culture and to seek equality with those leading nations which spend a considerable amount of money on cultural diplomacy.

The most influential organization involved in cultural diplomacy is the Japan Foundation, an adjunct of the Foreign Ministry established in 1972. The spending budget amounted in that year to ¥7.7 billion; the Foundation has a total staff of only 137 and 10 liaison offices overseas, compared to 120 overseas offices and 3,500 employees for the British Council and 148 overseas offices and 3,500 employees for the German Goethe Institute. The Cultural Affairs

Division of the Ministry itself had a budget of ¥2 billion in 1986, involving about fifty projects. The Japan Foundation is concerned with the exchange of scholars and artists, the organization of lectures, exhibitions, arts and sports encounters abroad and, because of the lack of financial means in Third World countries, the sponsorship of the introduction of culture from these states, especially Southeast Asia, into Japan. In addition it has made a great contribution to the expansion abroad of Japanese studies, notably Japanese language instruction.

On the initiative of Prime Minister Takeshita, a private advisory committee on cultural diplomacy was established in 1988 to review the existing pattern of activities, which had been criticized as being haphazard, piecemeal and hampered by bureaucratic red tape. In a major speech in London in May 1988, Takeshita called cultural diplomacy one of the pillars of international cooperation. It is now planned to expand cultural activities in Southeast Asia and Japanese language teaching worldwide. Several companies have made funds available for Japanese studies in foreign countries. The greatest share of this money has gone to the United States, followed probably by the United Kingdom, where Japanese studies departments in the universities of London, Oxford and Cambridge have been directly funded. Several overseas sports clubs are sponsored by Japanese companies. In 1988 the Keidanren set up a standing committee on international cultural exchange, in which about 500 Japanese companies offered to participate. In 1988 the government changed the tax law so that financial contributions for cultural and other public-interest purposes became tax-free. It can therefore be expected that Japanese companies will become much more visible in countries with substantial Japanese investment in order to prove themselves good members of the community. So far, it is true, most activities have been focused on the United States and this will remain unquestionably the principal target, followed by Europe, but the imbalance is to be altered somewhat by devoting more attention to Japan's Asian neighbours.

However, more than just the funding and planning of cultural diplomacy will have to change in order to enhance its impact and avoid the impression that it merely provides a fig-leaf for bad images created by Japan's economic activities abroad. Japan has to work harder than other nations to become accepted abroad because, for many non-Japanese, its economic expansion has followed too closely its pre-1945 military expansion. There is also the danger of actually widening the cultural gap by indulging in counter-productive and mistaken overemphasis on Japan's uniqueness. These problems are increasingly being recognized in Japan, and the involvement of more Japanese themselves in cultural exchanges will provide a counterweight. As the public financial resources of Japan's partners dry up, with an inevitable cutback in their external cultural activities, Japan can be expected to become more visible on the cultural diplomacy front.

Domestic influences

This overview of the domestic and historical background of Japanese foreign policy cannot fail to point out that Japan is still a relatively insular country. Historically developed perceptions and behavioural idiosyncrasies not only linger on, but are sometimes enhanced by a new self-consciousness and pride based on recent economic success. Although an increasing number of Japanese travel or stay abroad and the outside world has become much more tangible to a greater number of people, it is at the same time difficult to find young people to work abroad for their companies. The political system is still rather parochial, although the number of actors taking part in the process of formulating and deciding foreign policies is rapidly increasing. This has complicated and made more crucial the role of the Foreign Ministry, both as the centre of expertise on the outside world and as the coordinator and arbiter of conflicting interests.

As the following chapters will show, however, insularity and parochialism have not hindered the formulation of effective policies to cope with outside challenges. Until the 1970s the relative insulation of foreign policy from public concern – except over the issues of rearmament and Japanese-US security relations – had allowed a smooth aggregation of national interests and required only a minimal response to outside demands. However, in the 1980s Japan's increasingly prominent position in the global economy and the rapid changes in the international environment have made such minimal responses less acceptable.

4
NATIONAL SECURITY AND THE JAPAN-US RELATIONSHIP

This chapter examines Japan's new approach to the international politico-security environment, particularly as it has affected the crucial bilateral relationship with the United States. Japan's diplomacy up to the early 1970s had been based on the assumption that US protection and support could be taken for granted. To be sure, with Japan's growing economic success and trade expansion the national interests of Japan and the United States started to clash occasionally, but Japan's leaders believed that piecemeal concessions would always succeed in pacifying their partner. In the security area, it was assumed that a very gradual increase of defence expenditures would be sufficient to ensure the continuity of the two-track model; that is, Japan would be able to concentrate on the economy while the United States would take the ultimate responsibility for Japan's security. In exchange, Japan would support the major goals of American foreign and security policies and provide bases in Japan.

The changes in the international environment and in US foreign and security policies during the 1970s, however, threatened all these comfortable assumptions and demanded new responses from Japan. Its leaders realized they could no longer take the benign nature of the international environment for granted but would have to work to maintain it in the face of rapid political and economic changes. For example, Japan could do little to change the political causes of the oil crisis, but it did adopt a pro-Arab stance in 1973. For the first time Japan departed radically from its position of aligning with US positions on major issues and joined the West European countries in taking a more accommodating line on Arab demands.

Japan's leaders started to diversify the country's foreign policy and tried to improve relations with as many countries as possible. It was called 'omnidirectional diplomacy' (*zenhoi gaiko*). The government also felt freer to pursue a more active multilateral diplomacy after the United States had handed back Okinawa to the mainland in 1972. With the reversion of Okinawa, all pending issues from the aftermath of the war were resolved – except the intractable Northern Territories problem with the Soviet Union – and this reinforced the impression that Japan was standing at the beginning of a new age in its relationship with the rest of the world.

The concept of 'Comprehensive National Security'

Japan's most serious response to the changing international environment emerged in 1980 with the Report on Comprehensive National Security. The report was compiled by a study group instituted by Prime Minister Ohira Masayoshi, who had also set up other study groups to investigate Japan's economic relationships and the Pacific Basin Community idea. The report characterized the 'termination of clear American supremacy in both military and economic spheres' in the 1970s as a most fundamental change and stated that US military power was 'no longer able to provide its allies and friends with nearly full security'. According to the report, Japan had tended to preach a peaceful world while depending on others to do something to achieve it. The group suggested that the new situation required efforts on three levels: 'efforts to turn the overall international environment into a favourable one; self-reliant efforts to cope with threats; and as intermediary efforts, efforts to create a favourable international environment within a limited scope while protecting security in solidarity with countries sharing the same ideals and interests.'[3]

A number of ideas and concepts that had started to appear in Japan after the 1973–4 oil crisis were merged in the report, which marked a turning-point in Japan's postwar foreign and security policy. Although the term 'comprehensive security' is no longer in vogue, all Japanese governments since 1980 have based their responses on the analysis of the report and followed its recommendations with more or less vigour and success.

Two points in particular in the report have had a long-term influence: its dismissal of omnidirectional diplomacy, and its recommendation that the country's national security policy be integrated into an overall framework. The Ohira cabinet abandoned the short-lived post-oil-shock policy of omnidirectional diplomacy, which had never been credible and had only been criticized by Japan's Western allies as a mask for opportunism and the evasion of responsibility. As a signatory of the Japan-US Security Treaty, which the government always declared to be the basis of its security policy, Japan could not possibly conduct omnidirectional diplomacy and at the same time maintain equidistance from both superpowers. The 1978 Treaty of Peace and Friendship with China was clearly directed against the Soviet Union, and therefore Tokyo could no longer claim any shadow of doubt as to its position in the global rivalry between the superpowers. The Soviet invasion of Afghanistan and the US hostage crisis in Iran demanded a clear statement that Japan belonged to the West if it were not to risk diplomatic isolation.

The other major point, the declaration that national defence should be an integral part of Japan's security in the broadest sense, led to the formulation of the term 'comprehensive security'. This was defined as a policy to protect Japan against all sorts of external threats (the report itself also included countermeasures against earthquakes), through a combination of diplomacy, national defence, economic and other measures. The term thus freed Japan's national security from the straitjacket of the Security Treaty, allowing Japan to secure its external environment by other means, such as aid to strategically important countries, and transcending to some extent the sharp divide between the system of the Peace Constitution and the system of the Security Treaty.

Some Japanese criticized the concept of comprehensive security as being a smokescreen for increased military efforts, while others argued that it would divert attention from the necessity of increased military contributions. It was never made clear how the balance should be struck between the three pillars of diplomacy, national defence and economic measures (if, in fact, it is possible), but at least the concept of comprehensive security made it easier to elevate military efforts to a more or less equal rank beside diplomacy and economic measures. The greatest external support for this recognition came from China, which as far back as 1972, after the normalization of diplomatic relations, had not only stopped its warnings about the revival of Japanese militarism, but also acknowledged both the right of every nation to provide for its national security and the positive contribution of the Japan-US Security Treaty to regional security. This seriously weakened the domestic opposition on defence issues, notably the Japan Socialist Party, which could now no longer rely on support from China.

Security as the backbone of Japan-US relations

Japan's most important and intense relationship is with the United States. Chapter 2 described how the United States acquired its overriding influence over Japan's relations with the outside through its occupation of Japan and its hegemonic position in postwar Asia. Although the United States could not translate this position into an economic presence in Japan in the way that it gained a foothold through foreign investment in Western Europe, trade did contribute to the close bilateral relationship. Since the 1950s the United States has been Japan's most important trading partner, but it was the Security Treaty of 1951 and the revised treaty of 1960 which provided the backbone of the overall relationship. When the Japanese government asserts that the relationship with the United States is the cornerstone of Japan's foreign and security policy, this is nowhere more applicable than to the country's national defence.

According to the 1976 National Defence Programme Outline, the most recent official statement on national defence, the SDF is to repulse small-case aggression without external assistance. Anything more serious is to be countered in cooperation with US forces. For nuclear deterrence, Japan depends entirely on the US nuclear umbrella. Defence has thus become the centre-piece of the Japan-US relationship, and as long as such an essential element of national survival is linked to the United States, the bilateral relationship will dominate Japan's relations with the outside world and will relegate the relationship with other countries to a secondary place.

Deterrence is usually directed against external threats, which are to be met by military force only in the event of deterrence breakdown. Discussion of national security therefore normally concentrates on where the threat comes from and how it can best be countered with limited political, economic and technological resources. In Japan, however, public discussion has been dominated until very recently by the size of defence expenditures in relation to GNP and by how far Japan has to increase its defence efforts in order to manage Japan-US relations as a whole, and particularly growing economic frictions, so as to retain the US security guarantee. Yet it is very telling that the bilateral security link has often been isolated from the continuous and growing economic conflict between Japan and the United States in the 1980s.

Intensification of the security link

The Report on Comprehensive Security had proposed a 20% increase in Japan's defence expenditures in order to build up the country's own defence efforts and to reduce its reliance on the US Security Treaty. The USA's reaction to the changed international environment and its own relative decline provided sufficient pressure to prompt Japan to create a consensus on doing more for defence. The result has been more potent Japanese forces, but also a much more closely interwoven security partnership with the United States.

In 1980 Japan was publicly and strongly criticized by both the Secretary of State and the Defence Secretary of the United States for not raising its defence budget sufficiently. However, it soon became apparent that, at least in the defence sector, such 'Japan bashing' was not very constructive, so the Reagan administration finally adopted a policy of not criticizing its allies in public. Instead, it discussed defence cooperation on the basis of 'roles and missions' rather than on arbitrary statistical indices such as percentages of GNP. In March 1981, Defence Secretary Caspar Weinberger told the Senate Armed Services Committee that a rational division of labour among Japan, the United States and the NATO allies would be a central thrust of the administration's defence policy. Such an incremental approach was not easy at a time when US congressional resolutions were proposing much more radical measures, such as Japanese naval patrols to the Indian Ocean, revision of the Security Treaty, and a Japanese payment of a $20 billion security tax to the United States. The fruit of the administration's efforts was the separation of the defence issue from disputes emanating mainly from the trade area, as well as the further strengthening of bilateral defence cooperation and the integration of Japan's defence efforts into the US global deterrence posture. The underlying US assumption continues to be that since Japanese security is dependent on the global balance of forces and a war-winning capability on the part of the United States, Japan itself must take responsibility for more elements supporting such a posture.

On the Japanese side, there were a number of factors which made it possible to intensify the military relationship with the United States. First, there was public recognition of the harsher international security environment in the 1980s. Even recently, despite a new period of relaxation in East-West relations following the Intermediate Nuclear Forces (INF) agreement in December 1987, the Defence White Paper of 1988 still described the world situation as 'harsh, complicated and fluid'. US and Japanese government leaders have missed no opportunity to point out the expansion of the Soviet Pacific Fleet, continued tension on the Korean peninsula and the dependence of Japan on the security of the sea lanes. This has meant that increased defence expenditures and more operational military ties have become more acceptable. Second, in contrast to Western Europe, there was no disruptive public discussion over questions such as the stationing of land-based missiles, which would have endangered the change in public opinion towards defence. Third, there has been a growing recognition that Japan, with its new economic power, cannot confine itself to a mere economic role but has to make a greater commitment to its own defence as well as carry a larger share of the region's defence burden. Fourth, economic success and the Japanese perception of the relative decline of both the United States and Europe have boosted nationalistic feelings. Some Japanese consider that their country's national status will be recognized only if there is a commensurate military potential. Finally, in the face of ever-escalating economic frictions with the United States and the weight given by Japan's leaders to the economic relationship, the development of a more operational military alliance has been seen as inescapable.

More resources for the SDF

In Prime Minister Nakasone the Reagan administration found a partner who was willing to draw practical conclusions from the policy stating that Japan is part of the West and must contribute to common security. Although it was politically difficult, Nakasone managed to keep the average annual growth rate of defence spending after 1982 in excess of 5%, while the growth rates of most other budget items were severely curtailed in order to reduce the huge budgetary deficit. He effectively used US pressure and increased Soviet military activities in the region as well as elsewhere to convince a larger part of public opinion of the necessity for more defence efforts. The Soviet Union continued to increase its military forces around Japan and showed no flexibility on the issue of the Northern Territories. Diplomatic relations with Moscow, following the Soviet invasion of Afghanistan and the Vietnamese invasion of Kampuchea, reached freezing-point. Japan joined a US-sponsored boycott of the 1980 Olympics in Moscow, and economic sanctions against the Soviet Union were instituted after the invasion of Afghanistan. The Soviet Union voiced increased displeasure about Japan's closer defence cooperation with the United States and continued to consider Japan as merely an adjunct to its rival superpower. The defence budget tripled from ¥1093 billion in 1974 to ¥3137 billion in 1985. In 1987 the government decided to scrap the spending ceiling of less than 1% of GNP for the defence budget, which had been accepted policy since 1976. Although in the recent budget estimates that ceiling has been surpassed only to a very minor extent (1.004% in 1987 and 1.013% in 1988), the symbolic significance of this step was much greater. In fact, it turned out later that because of the growth in the Japanese economy in 1987 the defence budget never breached the 1% ceiling, but the psychological damage was already done.

In 1988 the defence budget rose to ¥3700 billion (at an exchange rate of ¥135 to the dollar this amounted to $27.4 billion), and the planned defence budget for FY1989 is ¥3900 billion ($28.8 billion). In terms of spending, this puts Japan roughly on a par with Britain, which ranks third after the United States and the Soviet Union. However, if the defence budget is calculated according to NATO yardsticks, the Japanese defence expenditures in 1988 amounted to $41 billion, the third highest in the world. The steep appreciation of the yen has brought more purchasing power for the SDF, which obtains its most sophisticated military equipment from the United States. As a result of its political will and economic strength, Japan has today a military capability which must be rated first-class in global, as well as regional, terms.

Japan has a total of only 246,000 active members in its armed forces – very low in relation to total population in comparison with other countries. However, the size of its ground forces, numbering 156,000, corresponds to Britain's (with 158,700). The members of all three services are volunteers and well trained. What has dramatically increased and improved Japan's defence power is the heavy focus on the procurement of state-of-the-art hardware. The Ground Self-Defence Force (GSDF) now has 1,150 tanks, the Maritime Self-Defence Force (MSDF) over 50 destroyers and 15 submarines, and the MSDF and Air Self-Defence Force (ASDF) together have 473 combat aircraft. Although the SDF still suffers from inadequacies, such as shortages in logistics, few reserve forces and problems with joint operations, the force constitutes in regional terms the most modern non-nuclear power in Asia. At the moment the Defence Agency is in the middle of implementing the goals of the National Defence Programme Outline. According to this plan, Japan will acquire 60 destroyers, 100 P-3C reconnaissance aircraft, and 200 F-15 Eagle fighters, and have its Nike-J missiles replaced by the Patriot system. In 1987 discussions were started to revise the quantitative goals of the plan.

Japan's military is also supported by a considerable arms production capability, which now accounts for the production of 90% of the SDF's equipment. Although aircraft and certain weapon systems and their electronic guidances are either imported from the United States or produced under licence, Japan is increasingly making use of its technological capability in the civilian sector to develop and produce high-technology weapons. This tendency is enhanced by the fact that Japan is particularly strong in electronics, which are such a key component of modern weapons. The 1988 Defence White Paper urged more intensive research and development of defence technology by fully utilizing the private sector's technological capabilities in microelectronics and the use of new materials.

Institutionalization of the security link
The regional and global importance of these defence efforts is enhanced and given a distinct direction by the intensification of Japan-US defence cooperation. The new age in this cooperation started in November 1978, when both countries agreed on guidelines calling for joint operational plans, including emergency planning, common procedures for cooperation in communications and logistic support, and more joint training. It may seem strange that under a bilateral security treaty which has been in force for over 25 years, both partners should agree so late on these kinds of issues, which are so vital for an effective defence alliance. However, this only serves to illustrate the constraints resulting from the two contradictory streams in Japan's foreign and security policy, as well as the military superiority which the United States enjoyed for so long.

It is also significant that the government, in deference to the political thinking associated with support of the Peace Constitution, officially claims that Japan has no right to collective defence and that any US help, if Japan were to be directly attacked, is different from the security arrangements of NATO. In 1981 the Japanese Foreign Minister actually had to resign after the Security Treaty was called an 'alliance' by Prime Minister Suzuki. It is a measure of the shift in domestic perceptions during the 1980s that the term has now become publicly accepted. In contrast to NATO, the Security Treaty places different burdens on each partner: there is an obligation for the United States to defend Japan, but not vice versa; instead, Japan has to permit the United States to use its forces in Japan not only for the defence of Japan but also for the security of the Far East.

The controversy within Japan over the scrapping of the 1% of GNP ceiling for the defence budget demonstrated the political difficulties in dismantling the many links that have been developed over the years between the two political streams. The Japanese government, therefore, prefers to proceed by changing or widening the interpretation of these constraints. Joint operational plans based on the guidelines are being worked out. They cover in particular actions in response to an armed attack on Japan and to 'a situation in the Far East outside of Japan which would have an important influence on the security of Japan'. Since any armed conflict in the region would have serious repercussions on Japan's security, this planning covers all conceivable contingencies, and, in particular, the occurrence of a new war on the Korean peninsula, the most volatile spot in the region. The details concern such matters as coordination of actions, allocation of tasks, logistical support by the Japanese and exchange of intelligence. Public discussion centres on the question of when and how far Japanese forces are allowed to help US forces in a situation where Japan is not under direct attack. One can safely assume that in the event of hostilities around Japan this question would be quickly dropped. The 1988 Defence White Paper also mentioned for the first time that the US military would cooperate with the SDF from the very beginning in the event of any attack against Japan, and not merely after independent efforts by the SDF had failed. In addition, joint exercises between the two countries are being increased and currently involve all three services, whose joint operations capability is not yet well developed. Since 1980 the Japanese MSDF has been taking part in the Pacific rim naval exercises (RIMPAC), which are held every two years in the Pacific; the United States, Australia, Canada and, occasionally, Britain take part. Nothing symbolizes better the growing defence cooperation and the departure from the past than the participation of the refurbished battleship *Missouri* in the RIMPAC exercises in 1988. It was aboard this ship in Tokyo Bay that Japanese and US leaders signed Japan's surrender documents in 1945.

At the same time the United States has upgraded its military presence in and around Japan. Being more distant from Asia than the Soviet Union, the United States has to rely on bases in foreign countries. Japan's location, in an arc in front of the Soviet maritime provinces, provides overall control of Soviet projections into the Pacific. The most important recent strategic move has been the deployment of Tomahawk cruise missiles on units of the Seventh Fleet since 1984. The opposition has attacked the government because of fears that these vessels might enter Japan and thus violate the third of the country's three non-nuclear principles – of not possessing, manufacturing or introducing nuclear weapons. However, public opinion, in the main, grudgingly accepts that nuclear weapons are part of the US security guarantee, while the government declares its trust that the United States will faithfully adhere to the third principle.

The US forces in Japan (USFJ) now number around 50,400. They use 105 military facilities (22 jointly with the SDF) and employ 21,700 Japanese. The United States, being largely a continental power, relies heavily on its navy to project its influence. The US marine corps has thus the largest contingent in Japan, with one aircraft carrier using Yokosuka, near Tokyo, as its home post. Thanks to bases in Japan, the Philippines and Diego Garcia, the US Seventh Fleet can operate between Hawaii and the Gulf. In view of the uncertain future of the US bases in the Philippines, the value of the Japanese bases may increase in the future. The US Air Force has close links with US bases in South Korea and plays an important role in maintaining the US deterrent on the peninsula. In 1985, the United States started to deploy two squadrons of F-16 fighters to Misawa, in northern Japan, from where they can reach the maritime provinces of the Soviet Union. Japan is increasing its financial support of the USFJ by paying up to half the labour cost of the Japanese workers on the US bases and by providing better facilities. A new labour-share agreement was concluded in 1987 and the government now plans a revision of the Stationing of Forces Agreement (SOFA). The annual financial support reached $2.5 billion in 1988, paying 40% of the annual $6 billion cost of the US forces in Japan; it is the most generous host-nation support per person anywhere from a US ally.

The defence of the sea lanes

The most controversial aspect of Japanese security policy, besides the scrapping of the 1% of GNP ceiling, was the announcement by Prime Minister Suzuki in 1981 that the SDF would secure two sea lanes, up to 1,000 nautical miles from Japan. It would seem natural that an island nation depending so much on the sea for its economic life should be concerned about the safety of these lifelines. However, only in the 1970s did the Soviet Pacific Fleet become a force to be reckoned with in the open sea. Today the Pacific Fleet has become the largest of the Soviet Union's four fleets, consisting of two aircraft carriers, 84 principal surface combatants, 120 submarines and 560 naval aircraft. The Fleet's primary operational mission is the protection of the Soviet Union's ballistic missile submarine force, based at Petropavlovsk in Kamchatka. Other missions growing in importance are the surveillance of the Chinese coast and US bases in the region, and, thanks to the use of bases in Indochina, the surveillance of the shipping routes through Southeast Asia.

In its strategic response to Soviet force development, the Reagan administration developed in the 1980s a new maritime strategy in which Japan occupies a central place. This strategy aims at deploying maritime forces as close as possible to the Soviet Union so as to strike the adversary at the earliest opportunity, prevent it from gaining access to the Pacific and render impossible the establishment of a sanctuary for Soviet nuclear submarines in the sea of Okhotsk. As an arc in front of the Soviet maritime provinces, Japan is the ideal staging ground for surveillance of Soviet activities as well as for forming a blockade against Soviet naval forces leaving for the Pacific. Soviet naval forces have to pass through at least one of the three straits of this arc in order to gain access to the Pacific Ocean: the Tsushima Straits between Korea and Japan's main island, Honshu; the Tsugaru Straits in the north between Honshu and Hokkaido; or the Soya Straits between Hokkaido and Sakhalin. Prime Minister Nakasone recognized the strategic importance of

Japan when he spoke of his country as a 'large aircraft carrier' during a visit to Washington in January 1983.

In response to the Soviet naval build-up and US urging, Japan has decided to modernize its forces in order to increase its capability for the protection and surveillance of its airspace up to several hundred miles and of its sea lanes up to 1,000 square miles. However, the government has been much more reluctant to agree publicly to a role in blockading the straits around Japan. Towards the end of Nakasone's premiership and under Takeshita, the government decided to introduce long-range Over-the-Horizon radar for early detection, long-range air defence improvements by enhancing the range of the F-15 fighters through the procurement of air tankers, and wide area ocean defence systems with AEGIS and DDG ships. Many resources have also been committed to improved anti-submarine warfare capabilities by procuring a larger number of P-3C aircraft.

Japanese public opinion, however, has not failed to be impressed by the Soviet withdrawal from Afghanistan and Mongolia, and the renewal of party-to-party relations between the Soviet Union and China. This development, as well as the weakening of the power of the LDP, will make it difficult to sustain a strong consensus to continue the enhancement of Japan's defence and military relationship with the United States. Nevertheless, public opinion in Japan has been less affected by the new Soviet policies than in Western Europe, and the instability in China, as shown in the bloody suppression of students in June 1989, has reminded the Japanese of the fragility of the regional system in East Asia.

In sum, the Japanese armed forces are involved in a major naval build-up which, in conjunction with US forces and their associated intelligence-gathering capabilities, will provide within a few years a much upgraded Western surveillance and interdiction capability in East Asia. The United States will increasingly rely on Japanese naval movements and air surveillance in order to reduce its costly physical military presence. The issue is to what degree the United States will want to continue to have the upper hand in these Japanese military activities and what degree of co-determination will be demanded by Japan, when the size of the military power of both countries in the region becomes reversed. In addition, both countries will have to counterbalance a more regional outlook on Japan's side with the more global US perspective of security. A new factor is the Soviet Union's reduced emphasis on military force and its intention to move to a more defensive military posture, albeit currently in Europe rather than in East Asia, where there is a more complex power constellation. Japan and the United States may well react differently to these new Soviet moves and this would influence the extent and progress of their military cooperation. Finally, the reaction of Japan's neighbours to this military build-up and the growing supplementation of US military power with Japanese forces needs to be considered.

Tapping the technological potential of Japan
A new dimension in the Japan-US security relationship is the role of high technology. Defence technology has always provided a link between Japan's economy and the Security Treaty since the conclusion in 1954 of the Mutual Defence Assistance Agreement, which played a positive role in helping Japan's industrial rehabilitation through the transfer of US defence technology. As Japan reached technological parity in many sectors, including some defence-relevant areas, the United States started to urge it to allow the flow of high technology to the United States. A bilateral agreement on military technology exchanges was concluded in 1983. As that ran against Japan's ban on arms exports, which dates back to 1967 and which was strengthened in 1976 by the inclusion of all military technology transfers, it took some time before the Nakasone government agreed to make an exception for the US ally. Through this agreement the United States wants to tap into Japanese high technology in order to maintain its own supremacy in military technology at a time of growing budgetary difficulties. From a European point of view it is regrettable that only the United States can use its influence in Japan to extract such advantages. This was demonstrated again in October 1987, when the Japanese government decided to renounce the option of indigenous development of a new support fighter and voted instead for the co-development of a

model based on the American F-16 fighter. Although the European Tornado was short-listed because of its qualities and the chance to reduce the dependence on American aviation technology, the Europeans had no comparable political weight. In this context it is worth noting that while the United States had a total trade deficit with Japan of $56.8 billion in 1986 (the total with the European members of NATO was $49.8 billion), it had, thanks to Japanese procurements, a surplus of $351 million in purely military trade with Japan (with NATO $1.7 billion).[4]

Other ways to access Japanese high technology were opened up by the United States with the conclusion of an SDI agreement in 1987, an understanding reached in January 1988 about Japanese participation in the Conventional Defence Initiative or Balanced Technology Initiative, and the participation of several major Japanese companies in the development of an anti-tactical ballistic missile system for the Pacific.

It is too early to judge the success of these agreements and plans. There are still major obstacles in the way. To the great embarrassment of the Departments of State and Defence, which had concluded the joint development of a fighter aircraft in November 1988, other US agencies, notably the Department of Commerce, demanded in January 1989 a review of the agreement because of the fear of losing sophisticated technology to Japan. The sale of the US AEGIS warship technology, involving a phased array radar, was bitterly opposed by some members in the US Congress. Producers in the United States are reluctant to let any part of the Pentagon's money and of their own high technology go abroad. The Japanese side is also anxious about losing technology to its chief competitor or becoming constrained by US requirements for secrecy, while the new administration of President George Bush is creating problems with its concern over protecting secrets and US industry.

Given the sensitivity of security issues in Japan's domestic political context, the evolution of the Japan-US security relationship over the last decade has been very remarkable. From a distant and reluctant ally, Japan has grown to be an ally which is closely coordinating with and increasingly supplementing US military roles, and has transformed its original limited national defence role into a regional security role. The present degree of coordination of both countries' military forces would have been unimaginable only ten years ago. Compared to the economic relationship (see Chapter 7), the security relationship seems to be on a sound footing, despite the continued burden-sharing grumbles of the US Congress. However, it will always be difficult to keep the frictions in the economic relationship permanently separated from those in the security dimension. The growing importance of high technology in international relations and particularly in the security field is pitting both countries against each other. Other challenges to the expanding bilateral security relationship are possible if Japan demands greater influence and/or autonomy in security matters because of its growing military strength, a weakening in the Soviet emphasis on military forces or the need for US military retrenchment owing to the budgetary deficit.

5
REGIONAL AND GLOBAL SECURITY

As the previous chapter has argued, the United States has remained central to Japanese foreign policy. However, the enhancement of Japan's globalist orientation during the 1980s has led to Japan paying greater attention not just to the Asian-Pacific region but also to Western Europe. Although it is difficult to separate economics from politics, this chapter will concentrate on the growing politico-strategic dimensions of Japan's interactions with these two regions, leaving the economic dimensions to be more fully covered in Chapters 7 and 8.

Intensification of Euro-Japanese relations
For Japan, Western Europe's importance lies in its economic weight (primarily as a market and investment site), its close links with the United States, and its role in the trilateral coordination of international affairs. During the postwar period, however, Europe's position has been overshadowed by the central role of Japan-US relations. Psychological barriers added to geographical distance: Japan faced considerable resentment in those West European states which had fought against it during the Pacific war, and the death of Emperor Hirohito in January 1989 demonstrated that these feelings still linger on in some quarters. When the EC was founded Japan suddenly became concerned about the possible emergence of an

economic bloc in Europe, and a flurry of diplomatic activity followed at the beginning of the 1960s. But since the consequences of the EC were less spectacular than Japan feared, this interest faded until the 1970s, when economic summitry brought both sides closer together. In the second half of the 1980s interest in Western Europe was heightened again because of the prospect of a single European market after 1992 (see Chapter 7).

Japan and Western Europe have discovered, however, that political dialogue and coordination are a necessary addition to their growing economic relationship. Both sides have come to the conclusion that common issues and divergent views can only be addressed by more direct consultation inside and outside the bilateral framework. In July 1978 Prime Minister Fukuda Takeo declared that 'the days are past when Japan and Europe could be content with an indirect relationship through the United States as an intermediary'.[5] The annual Western economic summit meetings have involved Japan side by side with Europe on major political and security issues, demonstrating to the Japanese that the European-US relationship can influence their own relations with the United States. Japan has realized that European support is needed if a consensus on contentious issues such as the Middle East conflict or the Soviet invasion of Afghanistan is to be reached. In 1988, Prime Minister Takeshita visited Europe twice; on the first occasion, in May, he announced his 'international cooperation initiative', designed specifically to boost cultural and political relations between Japan and Western Europe.

Japan is particularly interested in European views of the Soviet Union, Eastern Europe, the Middle East and Africa, whereas West European governments benefit from Japanese views on the Soviet Union in East Asia and the general political and military situation in East and Southeast Asia. Japan's growing international stature and its influence in its own region through trade, aid and investment have taken such exchanges of views and information beyond the level of mere courtesy calls. Japan, however, has been selective in supporting West European foreign policy approaches and is even less willing to sacrifice national economic interests than in its relationship with the United States. During Britain's confrontation with Argentina over the Falklands/Malvinas in 1982, Japan took a neutral position and popular sympathies in Japan were actually more with Argentina, where several thousand Japanese have settled permanently. During the controversy over Salman Rushdie's book on Islam in 1989 the Japanese reaction was rather subdued, reflecting Japan's considerable economic interests in Iran. On the other hand, it must be conceded that it is often not easy to side with the member states of the EC if they do not manage to find common ground on foreign policy issues among themselves.

Euro-Japanese relations are least developed in the security field, despite both sides being linked to the same superpower. West Germany was the first European country to signal to the Japanese that the two had similar interests in the defence area, when Helmut Schmidt, then Defence Minister, visited Japan in 1971. Because of the singular focus on the relationship with the United States and the sensitivity surrounding all security issues, the visit was only returned in 1978, by the Director-General of the Defence Agency. But since the beginning of the 1980s security issues have become standard fare for high-level meetings between European and Japanese government officials. In recognition of Japan's increased security role, the major West European powers have established regular bilateral security consultations with Japan. Since June 1980 Japanese parliamentarians have been invited as observers to the meetings of the North Atlantic Assembly, thus establishing an indirect link with NATO. Direct contacts between the Defence Agency and NATO headquarters in Brussels now take place regularly.

The most important issue in the security area is the East-West relationship, which was accentuated by the Soviet military build-up in the European and Far Eastern theatres, the invasion of Afghanistan and the Soviet support for Vietnam. However, the past ten years have highlighted differences in the ways in which East-West relations are perceived by Japan and Western Europe. The Soviet threat has been regarded as less ominous in Japan than in Europe because of the geographical difference and the sense of security nurtured by US military strength in the Far East. This still holds true, even though the Soviet Union is now considered to be a more potent threat to Japan's security. The Soviet Union's occupation of the so-called Northern Territories is very different from its military presence in Eastern Europe. The Soviet-held islands no longer have a Japanese population, whereas the West German government must always take into consideration possible Soviet retaliatory moves against East Germany, if its policies were to overly displease the Soviet Union.

These differences in circumstances and perceptions have made Japan less interested in pursuing detente policies independently. The Helsinki process was considered by Japan as detrimental to its own territorial conflict with the Soviet Union, because the West Europeans had accepted the territorial status quo in Eastern Europe. Japan did not enjoy the benefits of detente as directly as West Germany did, and it did not perceive a trade-off between detente and military confrontation in its own bilateral relationship with the Soviet Union. As a result it was more forthcoming in supporting the United States on the issue of economic sanctions and other retaliatory measures against the Soviet Union after the invasion of Afghanistan.

The reduced Soviet emphasis on military force since Mikhail Gorbachev's rise to power in 1985 has again demonstrated the differences between Japan and Western Europe in their approach to East-West relations. Arms control is not greeted with the same enthusiasm in Japan as in Europe. Japan is basically content with the existing strategic power constellation and does not favour any changes. It did not perceive the deployment of Soviet INF missiles as adding substantially to the Soviet threat, and it was not asked to receive ground-based US missiles to offset them. In the last analysis, the Europeans wanted counter-deployment in order to increase the US commitment to Western Europe. Whereas Japan considered a total elimination of all INF missiles as a matter of being treated equally by its Western partners, the Europeans (and the Reagan administration) were at one stage willing to accept a zero option for only the European part of the Soviet Union. Whereas most Europeans have embraced the new security policy of Gorbachev and are willing to respond to it by reducing their own military efforts and cooperating economically with the Soviet Union, Japan seems to be lagging behind, as it did during the heyday of the earlier detente period. But on other specific international security issues, such as international terrorism, the Middle East or Central America, Japanese and West European interests are very similar. Very often Japanese positions on these three issues are closer to those of the Europeans than those of the US administrations.

The development of the Japan-US security relationship has affected Japanese-European security relations in an ambiguous way. Japan and Western Europe are basically competing for US attention. Each side has at one time or another been fearful that during a crisis an overstretched United States might opt to help the other. The Japanese think that the historical and racial links between the United States and Europe might in the end swing the balance in favour of the Europeans, whereas the Europeans are concerned that the shift of US economic interests to the Asian-Pacific region will favour Japanese security interests. The feeling of competition may arise again as the new Bush administration begins to decide where to cut its military presence in order to rehabilitate its national finances.

On the other hand, an increased Japanese share of the defence burden in the Pacific is favourable for Europe's security, which is dependent on the maintenance of a global balance of power, and at the same time reduces US pressure on Europe to do more. There seems to be less ambivalence in Europe than in the United States about the possible consequences for the world power balance if Japan continues its present military build-up. West European security is also helped by a greater Japanese involvement in aid to strategically important countries surrounding Europe and by growing Japanese contributions to refugees (see below).

In sum, both Japan and Western Europe have discovered that their economic relationship has to be enhanced by a closer political and security relationship. Each needs the support of the other to advance its national interest. The international role of both sides in managing world politics has grown to such an extent that neither can rely any longer on the United States as an intermediary. The relationship between Japan and Europe, however, is least developed in the security field, which, in the absence of any agreement equal to the Japanese-US Security Treaty, will be limited to more coordination and more consultation.

Japan and the Asian-Pacific region

Since Japan opened up to the West in the mid-nineteenth century, it has grappled more or less continuously with the dichotomy of being both a part of Asia and part of the West. Since World War II, the Sino-Japanese ideological rift and Japan's orientation towards the other Western industrialized democracies have complicated Japan's relations with Asia. Nevertheless, there are three underlying factors which account for the distance between Japan and Asia: the opposition of democracy and authoritarianism, the contrast between wealth and poverty, and the legacy of Japan's past acts in Asia.

However, recent developments in the countries of the region are changing the divisive nature of these factors. Since the 1970s not only has the economic importance of East and Southeast Asia increased, but so also has its political and strategic weight. A number of capitalist countries such as South Korea, the Philippines and Taiwan have made progress towards more democratic politics, while several socialist countries are experimenting with economic, and even political, restructuring. The escalation of Japan's problems with its Western trading partners and the steep appreciation of the Japanese currency since 1985 have forced Japan to look to Asia for new opportunities. The economic development of the Asian-Pacific region has also given new vigour to regionalist policies, which will be discussed in Chapter 8.

(a) The Soviet-Japanese stalemate

Japan's most important adversary in Asia is the Soviet Union, whose aim in the postwar period has always been to break what it perceives to be a Western, that is, American, encirclement. There is obvious Soviet concern about Japan supplementing dwindling US military power at a time when the Soviet Union itself is trying to profit from the economic dynamism of the Asian-Pacific region. Much as the Soviet Union would like to see the close Japanese-US

49

military relationship dissolved, it appreciates, at the same time, the element of US control over Japan's expanding military power provided for by the Security Treaty. Japan has reacted very coolly to Gorbachev's overtures to the Pacific, in his speeches in Vladivostok in July 1986 and Krasnoyarsk in September 1988, and points instead at Soviet inflexibility on the issue of the Northern Territories.

In January 1986 Eduard Shevardnadze was the first Soviet foreign minister to visit Japan for ten years. However, no breakthrough was achieved and an agreement to resume the peace treaty negotiations did not take the relationship any further. The US-Soviet INF agreement in December 1987 had much less impact on Japan than on Europe because of the absence of land-based American INF missiles in East Asia. Indeed, the Japanese government particularly disliked the Soviet use of the issue to win popular support in Japan for opposition to the US bases there. It was symptomatic of Japanese preoccupations that the news about the conclusion of the agreement received no greater coverage in the media than an event that happened to coincide with it – the intrusion into Japanese airspace over Okinawa of a Soviet surveillance aircraft, at which Japanese aircraft for the first time in postwar history fired warning shots. Relations further cooled in the aftermath of the COCOM scandal in 1987–8, when the Japanese government had to prove that it was a loyal ally of the West by tightening restrictions on trade with the Soviet Union. Prime Minister Nakasone was keen to go to Moscow, but the Japanese Foreign Ministry considered that Gorbachev owed a visit to Japan first. The Soviet leader has been wary of undertaking such a trip as long as the main discussion item is likely to be the Northern Territories, without the prospect of a breakthrough in the economic sphere. Foreign Minister Shevardnadze's second visit to Japan in December 1988 was meant to prepare for a visit by Gorbachev in 1989, but domestic political uncertainties within Japan made it difficult to predict such an outcome. For the moment, the Japanese government's line is that a major compromise in the economic field (e.g. a long-term trade agreement) must be linked to Soviet accommodation of its territorial claim.

It will be very difficult for any government in Japan to eliminate the stumbling-block of the Northern Territories issue, because it is the only major foreign policy issue which has the full support of all parties and is strongly restrained by the Foreign Ministry bureaucracy. An ending of the stalemate may be more likely if a compromise on the territorial issue is seen as the final outcome of improved overall relations instead of the first step. During 1988, however, Soviet representatives tried to imply through various statements that Moscow recognized the need to do something about the territorial issue, which would be a departure from the hitherto held position that the issue no longer exists. If both sides continue to move along these new lines, a compromise will be possible and bilateral relations could improve.

Ultimately, however, what matters is the absence of any substantial material incentive for Japan to improve relations. The Soviet Union has high expectations of trading with Japan and attracting its capital and technology, but Japan lost interest in Siberian raw materials in the 1970s when it discovered their political and economic price. Improved relations could raise the suspicion of Japan's neighbours, including the United States, and give China a further incentive to strengthen its already improving relations with the Soviet Union. China may also see any compromise on the territorial issue as detrimental to the resolution of its own dispute with the Soviet Union over the exact position of the frontier along the Amur and Ussuri rivers. It is uncertain how Japan will react to a changing international environment of improved superpower relations, including a cut of 50% in strategic weapons, intensified contacts between the West Europeans and the Soviet Union, and further normalization of Sino-Soviet relations.

(b) China

From the establishment of diplomatic relations in 1972 until the beginning of the 1980s, China attempted to make Japan join its anti-hegemony campaign against the Soviet Union. Indeed, the Treaty of Peace and Friendship in 1978 even contained an article in which both parties vowed to oppose (unspecified) 'hegemony'. However, the Japanese government was anxious not to be drawn into this situation. There was also resistance to Chinese attempts to establish a level of Sino-Japanese military cooperation, because of Japan's concern over relations with Southeast Asia and the Soviet Union. Moreover, it is not in Japan's long-term interest to see China, its close neighbour, grow too big militarily and there are therefore some Japanese reservations about the declared US policy of help to modernize China's armed forces. In 1979 Prime Minister Ohira had excluded the extension of military assistance to China, so that military relations were limited to personnel exchanges; not until May 1987 did a Director-General of the Defence Agency make a visit to China. At the same time, however, the economic relationship has been developing; China now receives considerable assistance from Japan, which has helped the Chinese leadership to sustain economic reform and the opening towards the West. Since 1978 this has been Japan's main foreign policy goal in the relationship with China and has been presented by the government as an important contribution to regional and international stability.[6]

Until 1983 greater Japanese defence efforts and the strengthening of the security link with the United States were welcomed by China's leaders. The change in the Chinese attitude since then, shown by the resumption of publicly voiced concern about Japan's defence policy, can be attributed to several circumstances. First, the revived memory of Japan's aggression against China, through the textbook crises in 1982, 1984 and 1986, Japanese ministerial visits to the Yasukuni war memorial shrine, and the declarations by two cabinet ministers which played down Japan's wartime record. Second, the Japanese court decision which declared that a disputed student dormitory, Kokaryo, in Kyoto, belonged to Taiwan; this revived in Chinese eyes the spectre of a Japanese 'two-China policy'. Third, the abandonment of the 1% of GNP ceiling on Japanese annual defence expenditures in 1987. In 1980 China's Deputy Chief of General Staff, Wu Xiuqian, had intimated to Nakasone that Japan should increase its defence spending to the equivalent of 2% of its GNP; seven years later the Chinese Defence Minister advised the visiting Director-General of the Defence Agency that there should be a limit on Japan developing its defence forces in the 'light of the tragic lesson of history'.

Like other Asian countries, China now sees the expansion of

Japan's military potential as open-ended. As masters themselves in turning limited national power to maximum use, the Chinese leaders cannot imagine that Japan will abstain from translating this strength into at least political power to be used in international relations. Chinese attacks on the scrapping of the defence budget ceiling also betray a concern about the capability of the United States to check Japan's military role. Diplomatic incidents resulting from the memories of Japan's militaristic past reflect a genuine Chinese concern that Japan might forget its earlier misdeeds. At the same time, however, playing up incidents like the textbook crises and commemorating anniversaries of Japanese aggression also serve to exert pressure on Japan to offer greater or more generous economic engagement in China. Nevertheless, as will be analysed in Chapter 8, China's considerable dependence on Japan for its economic reconstruction creates difficulties of its own, and both problems are often presented as being linked because of Japan's alleged desire to dominate China.

(c) The two Koreas
Relations with South Korea have always been very delicate because of the legacy of Japan's occupation of the peninsula from 1910 to 1945. Accordingly, the textbook crises, the statements by cabinet ministers on Japan's imperialistic past and the official visits to the Yasukuni shrine have caused the same degree of uproar there as in China. In addition, South Korea is concerned about the treatment of a considerable Korean minority living in Japan. On the other hand, South Korea cannot ignore the important role which Japan, as host to a sizeable US military force, plays in its own security. Although both countries have a military alliance with the same superpower, the delicate overall relationship does not allow for direct military cooperation. Nevertheless, visits of military personnel have become regular, at least in the 1980s.

Because of South Korean sensitivities and Japan's heavy economic involvement in the South Korean economy, the Japanese government feels that it cannot do much to contribute to a lessening of tensions on the Korean peninsula. A normalization of relations with North Korea is therefore very difficult as long as the South

Korean government does not agree to it and the North Korean government continues to be inflexible on bilateral issues. Japan's role was made more difficult after the North Korean terrorist attack on President Chun and his entourage in Rangoon in 1983 and the destruction of a KAL airliner by a bomb in 1987. In both cases Japan had been used to some extent by the North Korean terrorists. In part that persuaded the Japanese government to play an important cooperative role with the South Korean government in ensuring security for the 1988 Seoul Olympic Games.

Japan's economic relationship with South Korea has contributed to the resilience of that country and has helped it to become one of the NIEs. South Korea, despite a per capita income of over $2,000, still receives considerable Japanese development aid, which is only explicable in terms of the country's strategic importance to Japan. Nakasone's unprecedented visit in 1983 opened a new chapter in the bilateral relationship by implicitly recognizing its strategic dimension. However, since Roh Tae-Woo's election as president and the National Assembly elections in April 1988, more South Korean expressions of dissatisfaction and concern about Japan's national defence posture have been heard. As in the case of China and Southeast Asia, it is often difficult to discern how far these criticisms are motivated by economic grievances. But the move to greater democracy in South Korea will in the long term eliminate from Japanese-South Korean relations the democracy/ authoritarianism divide. In addition the economic divide is likely to lose much of its abruptness. However, South Korea is still very anxious about any Japanese role in its foreign policy initiatives. When a high-ranking Japanese politician suggested in 1988 that Japan might act as a go-between in the growing Korean-Chinese relationship, South Korean reaction was very negative. The South Koreans prefer Japanese government leaders, in consultation with them, to confine themselves to raising the Korean situation at summit meetings in order to obtain the understanding of the other Western leaders.

(d) ASEAN and the South Pacific
The Southeast Asian countries have also expressed concern over

Japan's increase in military efforts in the light of the scrapping of the 1% of GNP ceiling and Japan's attitude towards its imperialistic past. Even Singapore, which has most approved of greater Japanese defence efforts, has become less sanguine about the open-ended nature of Japan's defence build-up. However, very often, demonstrations of concern in the security area are either nourished by economic grievances or used merely as a means of applying pressure on Japan for more political and economic support. Further economic development may also give the most important countries of the region more self-confidence in the face of growing Japanese power.

Yet the Southeast Asian countries are genuinely reluctant to see Japan patrol sea lanes too far away from Japan itself, as was demonstrated by their reactions in May 1988 when US Navy Secretary James Webb suggested that Japan should defend the sea lanes up to the Indian Ocean. They are particularly worried that the United States may hand over its regional security responsibilities to Japan. This concern may become very acute in the next few years, as the United States will have to cut back its military commitments in order to fight the budgetary deficit.

Japan's response has been both rhetorical and practical. The government stresses in every statement on foreign policy that Japan will never become a 'great military power' (*gunji taikoku*). Given Japan's growing military potential, however, it does not seem to be very clear for Japan's neighbours where the Japanese will draw the line. Since quantitative and qualitative restraints have proved to be of a temporary nature, it can only mean that Japan will not use military power in order to advance its national interests. In effect the Japanese government is referring to a range of limitations on the military, such as the renunciation of ICBMs, long-range strategic bombers and offensive aircraft carriers, as well as nuclear weapons, together with certain organizational features, such as the civilian control of the SDF and the maintenance of a merely voluntary armed force. In 1988, the Director-General of the Defence Agency visited the ASEAN region for the first time to soothe the fears of Indonesia and Singapore, in particular, about Japan's growing military power. On the practical level, there have been government attempts to prove Japan to be a good Asian neighbour, for example by supporting ASEAN's stance on the Vietnamese invasion of Cambodia and Laos, by bringing ASEAN's concerns into the international arena, through the economic summit and similar meetings, and by devoting considerable development aid to ASEAN. The economic dimension of Japan's growing role as a spokesman for the countries of the region will be considered in Chapter 8.

The enhanced presence of the Soviet Union in the South Pacific, through various fishery agreements and diplomatic representations, has raised the level of Japanese attention paid to this region in recent years. This heightened interest, also evident in the United States, has prompted Japan to try to contribute to a continued Western orientation for the island countries. It has, therefore, increased economic assistance, and Foreign Minister Kuranari Tadashi visited the area in 1987 to express Japan's political interest. He announced in Fiji five principles of Japanese policy towards the South Pacific, including support for regional cooperation in the area, assistance in preserving the stability of the Pacific island region and increased economic aid. Japanese ODA funds to the South Pacific island nations increased from $24 million in 1985 (1% of total ODA) to $68 million (1.3%) in 1987. In a radical departure from its traditional policy, the Japanese government contributed in 1987 for the first time to a national budget by allocating funds to the Tuvalu Trust Fund. Dialogue on the region was also put on an official level with Australia and New Zealand in 1985, with the United States in 1987, and with France and the United Kingdom in 1988.

New areas of comprehensive national security

Faced with demands from its Western allies for a greater share of the burden, Japan has become involved in many areas related to security where in the past it had been absent or had played only a minor role, such as aid to strategically-situated countries, refugee support, arms control and support of UN peace-enhancing activities. This expansion of Japan's burden-sharing, initiated in the early 1980s, was continued by Prime Minister Takeshita under the slogan of 'Japan contributing to the world', and is likely to continue into the 1990s.

(a) Strategic aid

In FY 1988 Japan surpassed the United States, the previous largest aid donor, in budgeted overseas development aid, with $10 billion approved for the year (see Chapter 6 for the economic aspects of this development). Japan has been motivated to do more after its leaders realized that rising conflicts in Third World countries have a negative impact on developing countries as raw material suppliers and as markets and constitute a threat to the maintenance of a peaceful international system. Japan discovered that development aid was a useful and acceptable means of influencing global and regional stability. Japan's aid during the 1980s, therefore, has gained more political overtones and has been concentrated more on regions or countries which have strategic importance not only for Japan but also for the West. Such aid has been called 'strategic aid'. Since the second half of the 1970s Japan has given significant aid to such diverse countries as Egypt, Oman, Sudan, Zimbabwe, Somalia, Kenya, Turkey, North Yemen, Pakistan and Jamaica, in addition to states in its own region, which still receive the largest amount of aid – principally China, South Korea and the ASEAN countries.

Aid to the Southeast Asian nations began with reparations in the 1950s and 1960s and has always had a political importance, quite apart from the economic rationale. From the beginning of the 1970s Japan started to use economic assistance as a means of applying sanctions, such as in the cases of the Socialist Republic of Vietnam, Kampuchea, Cuba, Angola, Afghanistan and Ethiopia. Similarly, aid provided political encouragement to the Philippines after the fall of President Ferdinand Marcos and to Afghanistan after the withdrawal of Soviet troops. Until 1988 Japan and West Germany were the largest aid donors to Burma. When the economic and political situation in Burma worsened in the summer of 1988, Japan promised increased aid only if the government chose a more realistic economic policy and opened the country to foreign investors.

Both the defence and the aid budgets have been exempted from the recent fiscal austerity policy favoured in Japan for the overall budget. This indicates their strong link with Japan's comprehensive security. Economic aid became in the 1980s a means of supplementing defence efforts, which for political as well as technical reasons could not be as easily increased as financial flows to the developing countries. The United States still plays the leading role in regional defence as a whole, but Japan is clearly taking over the dominant economic role in certain countries such as the Philippines. Faced with higher rental fees demanded for the maintenance of its bases in the Philippines, the United States is relying in part on Japan to resolve the issue by stepping up its own economic aid to the Philippines.

Along with other Western countries, Japan has strategic interests in the Gulf. However, in strictly military terms, it is restrained from military intervention by the system of the Peace Constitution. During the second oil crisis of 1979–80 the Foreign Ministry went as far as declaring that the Constitution would allow Japan to give financial assistance for the establishment of a multilateral fleet to protect the passage through the Straits of Hormuz. During the Gulf crisis in 1987 international pressure mounted on Japan to make a more sizeable contribution to security in the Gulf. It appears that Prime Minister Nakasone was willing to consider sending a minesweeping force, but in the end domestic opposition ruled this out. Instead, the Japanese government promised to give $10 million for the construction of a navigation system in the Gulf and to step up economic assistance to the countries in the region. Moreover, Japanese willingness to increase its host-nation support for US forces in Japan must be seen as related. Since Japan maintains full diplomatic relations with both Iran and Iraq, where it has substantial economic interests, Japanese officials have frequently visited both countries in order to enhance mutual understanding, and have supported UN efforts to bring about a peace settlement. Japan has also increased its economic aid to one key Middle Eastern country, Egypt, helping it to gain more foreign currency by supporting the enlargement of the Suez Canal. This was, incidentally, also a Japanese contribution to Western security, since it enabled US aircraft carriers to pass through the canal.

Traditionally, Africa has been largely absent from Japanese

concerns. However, since the mid-1980s perceptions have been changing. Pressure from Western allies, notably the United States, media reports on widespread famine (which prompted a campaign to raise funds for Africa), and lobbying by the anti-apartheid African states have all played a part. Japan has been conducting a lively economic relationship with South Africa, although it has heeded the critical voice of international public opinion by refusing normal diplomatic relations and curtailing sporting and cultural contacts. To the great embarrassment of the government, in 1987 Japan surpassed the United States as the leading economic partner of South Africa (with total trade of $4.27 billion), after many US companies had withdrawn from open involvement in the country.

In sum, although the United States still has considerable military means at its disposal around the world, the increased Japanese development aid amounts to a further relative eclipse of West European influence outside Europe as well as within international aid agencies. Nevertheless, Japan is short of expertise and manpower in order to dispense its aid money and has therefore to rely not only on Americans but also on Europeans. European security interests are also benefiting from Japanese aid, in so far as Japan is stepping up its support of countries and regions of immediate concern to Europe, such as the provision of aid to African states or the inclusion of Yugoslavia within its $30 billion surplus recycling programme.

(b) The refugee problem

Japan's policy towards refugees is closely linked to strategic aid. Among its aid beneficiaries are countries such as Pakistan, Thailand, Sudan and Somalia, which are all threatened by destabilization because of the influx of refugees. When refugees started to flood into Southeast Asia from Vietnam after 1975, Japan was harshly criticized for not accepting refugees itself. In July 1981 the Japanese government made its point of view clear, declaring that it considered the refugee problem not only a humanitarian issue but also a major political issue affecting peace and stability in Southeast Asia. By December 1987 only 5,400 Indochinese refugees had been permanently settled, but rather than accepting refugees itself, which was considered to be socially and politically too difficult (actually few want to stay in Japan), the Japanese government has concentrated on financial support for the UN High Commissioner for Refugees (UNHCR) as well as for other organizations involved in resettlement, and on exerting pressure on Vietnam to restrain outflows of people. Now Japan's contributions account for over 50% of the UNHCR budget, amounting to $47 million in FY 1986, of which about half went to help Indochinese refugees. However, Japan cannot expect full credit from its Western partners for its refugee help as long as it is seen to be buying itself out, while other countries accept the refugees in their midst and suffer social strains as a result.

(c) *Arms control*

Japan's first major involvement in arms control occurred with the nuclear Non-Proliferation Treaty (NPT), which it ratified after a long debate in 1976. What was at stake for Japan, as in the case of West Germany, was not so much the foreclosure of the nuclear option, but the need for uninhibited use of nuclear energy and for equal treatment with other Western nations over safeguards. However, it was the INF issue which really highlighted for the first time the importance of East Asia in arms control negotiations, which had previously in the main focused on either the superpowers or Europe. For Japan, it was not so much its own security which mattered, but its membership of the Western camp and the notion of indivisible security in the trilateral world. At one point during the negotiations the United States, with the support of West European leaders, had created the impression that it would settle for an agreement which would move SS-20s directed against Western Europe to the Far East. It is for this reason that Prime Minister Nakasone, to the surprise of most Japanese and foreign observers, endorsed the 1983 Williamsburg economic summit declaration that the 'security of our countries is indivisible'.

In other arms control issues, Japan's stature is rising because of its economic and technological strength. It is active in contributing to the conclusion of a complete test ban and a ban on chemical weapons in the Geneva Conference on Disarmament. In 1987 Japan joined the other economic summit nations in an agreement to ban the transfer of certain missile technologies. These developments mean a maturation of Japan's arms control policy, dominated until the 1970s by declaratory policies which were mainly directed at the reconciliation of the two political streams mentioned earlier, by invoking the memory of the atom bombs dropped on Hiroshima and Nagasaki and by stressing that Japan was a country devoted to peace (*heiwa kokka*). Only in 1980 did the Suzuki cabinet publicly recognize that 'disarmament and national security are two sides of the same coin'. At the same time, however, Suzuki circumscribed Japan's room for manoeuvre in the arms control field and stressed the validity of the concept of the balance of power in its arms control statements. Prime Minister Takeshita added in June 1988 that arms control must take regional characteristics into account and that it required transparency of military information and effective verification. This further aligned Japan with the Western and, in particular, the US arms control position. Moreover, Takeshita did express Japan's reservations about a transfer of the Helsinki process to East Asia, as has been proposed by the Soviet Union on various occasions since 1969; the Japanese government considers this to be fundamentally detrimental to its territorial claim towards Moscow over the Northern Territories.

(d) Reinvigorating UN peace-enhancing activities
Membership of the United Nations in 1956 raised great expectations in most Japanese. It was welcomed both as a symbol of Japan's readmission to the world and as a guarantee against the recurrence of Japanese militarism. Japan's first diplomatic Blue Book in 1957 tried to combine this national enthusiasm with a *realpolitik* approach, when it defined the three guiding principles of Japan's diplomacy as a UN-centred diplomacy, cooperation with the free nations and re-establishment of membership of the Asian community. In fact, because of its strict alignment with US policies and reluctance to come up with initiatives, Japan's role in the United Nations was very subdued. Owing to its SDF law, which does not allow the dispatch of military personnel abroad, Japan could not even take part in Peace-Keeping Operations (PKO).

However, when faced with the need to contribute more to the

maintenance of a peaceful environment at the beginning of the 1980s, Japan saw increased activity in the UN as offering one of the least delicate means, in political terms. In addition, it had the advantage of appealing to the Third World, which had been a major constituency of Japan's foreign and security policy since the early 1970s. Alarmed by the crisis in the United Nations, in 1985 it proposed a group to consider ways of making the United Nations more efficient. Meanwhile, Japan's voluntary and regular contributions to UN activities increased steadily, and more Japanese personnel joined the secretariat. In 1982 the government proposed to strengthen the UN peace-keeping functions, to which it had financially contributed. This necessarily brought further impetus to the issue of Japanese personnel involvement, which was opposed by those who fear the softening or even revision of the SDF law. In view of Japan's enhanced military posture, however, there is also concern about misinterpretation by countries suspicious of Japan's new military muscle. In 1988 Japan allowed a diplomat to participate in the truce supervision team for Afghanistan, and it seems that the dispatch of civilian personnel in fields such as the supervision of elections, transportation, communication and medical services is possible. In April 1988 Japan did make a special contribution of $20 million for the PKO in Afghanistan, the Gulf and Lebanon. Other Japanese measures concern efforts to foster dialogue between fighting parties, either independently or in collaboration with the United Nations.

It becomes apparent, therefore, that while Japan's political and security policies still revolve mainly around the United States, the country has become a major international player which is gradually translating its economic power into political influence in every corner of the world. At the same time, its military potential looms larger than ever on the horizon. Although it is still firmly integrated into the alliance with the United States, Japan is increasingly supplementing US military power in Asia, and the United States is encouraging it to play a more active political role in promoting the process of Asia's economic and political development. Japan is devoting more attention to this growing Asian environment, from which is no longer so sharply divided. The recent increase in

Japanese attention to Western Europe, and the expansion of political and security consultation and coordination, also indicate that Japan is no longer just an economic competitor but is likely to become a political challenge to Europe's influence on the stage of world politics.

6
ECONOMIC POWER

The earlier chapters have shown that Japan's leaders have so far been rather circumspect about translating even economic – let alone military – power into political influence on the outside world. However, there have been fewer inhibitions about further increasing this economic power and playing a correspondingly greater role in the international market for goods and raw materials. These leaders generally considered that this could be done without major political involvement. Yet this attitude ignored the fact that Japan's economic outreach alone, in terms of both raw material imports and market share of international products, would exert a political influence on other countries, particularly those in an economically weak position.

In addition, the changes in the international environment since the 1970s have shown that Japan has to use political power, accruing from its overseas economic involvement, in order to sustain the global free-trade economic system on which it depends, and has to contribute to the international management of that system. In view of the relative decline of other Western powers, rising economic frictions with its most important Western partners and an economy whose share of world GNP, in dollar terms, has reached 13%, pressure has been applied on Japan to take more of the burden from others in maintaining the world economic system. Although all its partners agree that it should contribute more to the management of the international economic system, there is disagreement as to what exactly Japan should do, and ignorance about the consequences. Few realize that greater Japanese burden-sharing will actually reduce their own power relatively, in terms of determining the future of the world economic system. The question is particularly relevant for Western Europe, since the outcome of the race for economic power will determine its standing in world politics in the future.

Japan's economic strength
What are the links between Japan's economy and the world economy? One important fact is that Japan is a country with a population of 122 million, which imports most of its raw materials and energy requirements. Somewhat surprisingly, the degree of Japan's involvement and integration into the world economy is actually rather low compared to most other Western countries, because of its large internal market and low import propensity. Japan's external trade is low in terms of its population (in 1987, exports totalled $233.39 billion and imports $139.11 billion), so the ratio of its foreign trade to its huge GNP is also low. In 1986, the ratio was 10.7% for Japan's exports and 6.5% for its imports. For West Germany, France and Britain the figures were 29.1% and 25.1%, 20.0% and 21.1%, and 22.1% and 23.8% respectively. Only the United States has comparably low ratios.

Although these figures cannot diminish the absolute necessity of trade for Japan's survival, they do have an impact on the Japanese perception of the relevance of the external world, and they complicate bilateral trade disputes based on Japan's trade surpluses and the mix of its import and export commodities. Moreover, these figures say nothing about the crucial role of exports in the growth of the Japanese economy and the continuing, and in some cases growing, need to import raw materials and food commodities. In addition, the very size and structure of its economy has made Japan the world's largest importer of many raw materials; this is of great importance not only to the exporting countries concerned, particularly those developing countries which are dependent on only a few export items, but also to all other countries which need to import the same raw materials.

Another indicator of Japan's involvement in the world economy is foreign direct investment. The FDI flow reached $33.36 billion in FY 1987, up 49.5% over the previous fiscal year. By international comparison, other foreign investors like the United States and Britain have much larger foreign investments, but the speed of growth of Japan's FDI is remarkable. Nevertheless, only 5% of the products of Japanese companies were manufactured abroad, compared to about 20% in the case of the United States. As in the case of trade there is an imbalance in investment: FDI into Japan in 1986 totalled only $7 billion, nearly three-quarters of that in the manufacturing sector (almost half of the FDI is from the United States).

As a result of its current-account surplus, Japan has become the world's most important capital exporter. Japan's surplus on the current-account balance of payments reached $84.54 billion in 1987, more than double the peak level of Saudi Arabia's surplus, in 1979, of $41.4 billion. At the end of 1987, thanks to the increasing trade surplus and the spectacular appreciation of the yen, Japan's net assets abroad had nearly doubled to $240.7 billion from $129.8 billion in 1986, making it the world's largest creditor nation for the third consecutive year. Between 1982 and 1986, Japan's gross external assets trebled to $727 billion. In 1987, Japan's net income from dividends and interest on foreign investments, $19 billion, for the first time surpassed the net receipts of the United States, making Japan the world's leading investment income earner (United Kingdom £5.7 billion). In 1986, foreign securities investment, which had been liberalized completely since April 1984, went first to the United States (49% of total, $49.6 billion), followed by Luxembourg, in Eurobonds (24%, $24.3 billion), and Britain (13%, $12.8 billion). The Japanese stock market is now the world's largest in terms of aggregate value of listed stocks, having overtaken New York in April 1987. In 1989 the ten largest banks in the world – ranked by deposits and equity-capital growth – were for the first time all Japanese. In terms of assets, the top Japanese banks had in 1987 a 35% share of the global market, up from 26% in 1985, whereas the

US share has fallen over the same period from 23.4% to 15.8%. The size of the assets, coupled with the revaluation of the yen, are driving Japan's investments abroad. The impact is felt everywhere. Thus Japan has made the transition from a trading giant in the 1970s to a financial giant in the mid-1980s in a much shorter time span than either Britain or the United States, which took decades to complete equivalent economic transformations.

As a result of its financial power Japan has also become a major player in all fields of financial speculation, ranging from currency speculation to participation in futures markets. Many Japanese companies have discovered that they can often make quicker profits in these fields than in manufacturing and trading of goods. This has contributed to wider fluctuations in world financial markets and increased instability. The behaviour of Japanese actors, with their enormous financial power, can be critical in a crisis situation, as was demonstrated in the stock-market crash in 1987.

This extremely rapid change in the degree of involvement in the world economy has exacerbated Japan's trade conflicts. Japan is faced with demands not only to rectify trade and investment imbalances, but also to change its economic structure from one that is focused on exports to one that gives similar importance to a wide range of imports. There is the implicit assumption that Japan would not be where it is now had it abided by the rules. It is accused of concentrating its exports on a limited though permanently changing gamut of goods (the 'laser approach'), having a low ratio of manufactured goods in its total imports (36.1% in 1986, compared with 62.5% for the total OECD area), being imbued with a spirit of total market control, and closing its market to foreigners. In addition, Japan is increasingly viewed as not only having out-performed many of its competitors in traditional industries such as steel and cars, but also of being on the point of making a successful transfer to the high-technology fields of the future, including electronics, new materials and space, as well as their applications in areas like communications and the service sector. Yet the same countries that criticize its trade as adversarial and its technological advance as dangerous for national security also expect Japan to contribute to the maintenance of the international economic system in the widest sense.

Participation in global economic management

Before looking at Japan's economic relations with its major trading partners, it is useful to examine how Japan is contributing to the maintenance of the international economic system on a multilateral level and how its economic structure has been changing so as to make it better integrated into the world economy.

Since the oil crisis in 1973, consultation and coordination on the management of international economic affairs between the major Western economic powers has increased. While at the beginning developments in oil prices dominated discussions, the issues now are rising protectionism, monetary instability, economic crises and the debt problem of the Third World. Many issues are linked to the relative decline of the United States and its inability to act with the same effectiveness as in the past. The United States, therefore, has come to rely on its other Western partners as well as a host of new international fora apart from the established multilateral organizations such as the GATT and the OECD, where international economic issues can be discussed. Japan, once a 'silent' observer, is now a member of most of these fora and is increasingly taking initiatives on its own.

The highest international forum is the annual economic summit, of which Japan has been a member since its beginning in November 1975. Although experiencing a relative decline of its power, the United States is still the driving force in the discussion on international economic policies, as the Japanese are well aware. As a result, Japan's policies towards these multilateral fora display both bilateralist and multilateralist approaches. One major US demand is for Japan and West Germany to stimulate their economies in order to become locomotives for the world economy. However, America's partners consider that this would not bring much benefit worldwide so long as the United States does not reduce its budget deficit and increase production. Because the United States considers a greater liberalization of world trade as the best solution to all problems, it initiated at the 1984 London summit, with the support of the Japanese government, another GATT trade liberalization round, the so-called Uruguay round. Reagan and Nakasone had agreed in November 1983 on the new GATT round at a time when the EC still opposed such a move as being precipitate.

Under the new round, the major US targets are the opening of the service and agricultural markets. In view of its strong dependence on trade and the economic relationship with the United States, Japan supports the general idea of trade liberalization, but, for reasons of economic autarky and LDP politics, it does not accept the far-reaching US demands on agricultural liberalization. The Uruguay round has become a major Japanese preoccupation. The problem is that other countries consider that highly advanced powers like the United States and Japan will in the end profit most. Japan has the best pre-conditions for quick adaptations to its industrial structure, a capability which will become even more necessary when trade is further liberalized. Extended liberalization of trade, therefore, will create problems for those countries which are not able, for economic and social reasons, to undertake the necessary fast pace of industrial change, or which want to protect less competitive service sectors and their fledgling high-technology sectors.

Of course, demands for greater Japanese participation in international economic organizations have to be matched by changes within these institutions themselves. Japan has become less hesitant, after having been reminded so often of its responsibility as the second largest economy in the world, about using its power in order to increase its influence in these multilateral institutions. As a result, the bilateralist orientation, towards both the United States and Western Europe, often suffers; increased Japanese burden-sharing means not only a relative reduction of their burden but also reduced voting power. In 1988, for example, Japan proposed a special increase of capital for the Asian Development Bank (ADB), which would imply greater voting rights. (The ADB has enough money but not enough borrowers, and Japan's proposal was motivated by its search for ways to recycle its $30 billion in surplus funds and to increase its influence in the bank, to which it is the largest contributor, if one includes the soft loans which are not taken into consideration when determining voting rights.) In the end both Japan and the United States have increased their capital, and thus their voting power, by the same margin. Since the early 1980s Japan has struggled to have its voting power extended at the World Bank and has used increased contributions to a special fund for the poorest countries as a lever. However, the World Bank example also illustrates that money and voting rights alone cannot by themselves reflect the economic strength of a country: in 1987 there were only 55 Japanese among the professional staff of the Bank, compared with over 100 from the United States.

Economic restructuring since the Plaza agreement
Nothing has changed more quickly the foundation of Japan's export-led economy than the dramatic decline of the dollar and the simultaneous rise of the yen, which has had important repercussions on the country's foreign policy. In reaction to the complaints from its trading partners concerning Japan's low import propensity and difficult market access, between 1981 and 1985 the government presented seven so-called 'market-opening packages'. The immediate impact of these measures has hardly been encouraging and their future effectiveness is somewhat limited. In the summer of 1985 the government launched a three-year action programme to promote imports into Japan more aggressively. For the first time the government officially declared that imports were 'good', when Nakasone went on TV and urged his countrymen to buy foreign products. In addition, the government stimulated domestic demand through changes in regulations and public investment programmes. In the same year Nakasone established a private advisory commission, which came to be known as the Maekawa Commission, to examine restructuring issues. The Maekawa Report, delivered in April 1987, demanded a stimulation of domestic demand, deregulation and restructuring of the industrial set-up in order to attain the goal of reducing the current-account imbalance to one 'consistent with international harmony'. It demanded a basic transformation in Japan's trade and industrial structure, from export-orientation to import-orientation. Although some foreign observers expected

Table 1 US current-account and trade deficits with Japan
(US$) billion)

Year	Current account	Trade balance
1983	−19.8	−21.1
1984	−37.8	−37.1
1985	−45.2	−43.5
1986	−56.1	−54.4
1987	−58.5	−57.0

Source: US Department of Commerce, Bureau of Economic Analysis.

immediate changes, the Maekawa Commission clearly thought that
these processes would take time to introduce.

However, the appreciation of the yen against the dollar since 1985
has hastened the process of restructuring enormously and dampened
down many domestic forces opposed to any further opening of the
Japanese market. In September 1985, the Group of Five key
currency countries agreed on the devaluation of the US dollar and
revaluation of the yen in what has become known as the Plaza
agreement. From a level of ¥230 to the dollar at the time of this
agreement, Japan's currency soared to ¥144 at the end of 1987 and
¥128 in January 1989. The dramatic effect of the yen appreciation
has been not so much on the quantity of Japan's exports as on their
composition. Because of the so-called J-curve effect, the currency
change did not immediately result in a drastic reduction of the
Japan-US trade imbalance but actually enhanced it (see Table 1).
However, the costs associated with the rise of the yen forced
Japanese industry to abandon the production of certain goods, shift
some production to other countries, and enhance manufacturing
efficiency through automation and other means. First signs of the
changes to the trade structure can be observed from the fact that
almost half of the imports by value are now manufactured goods
(44% in 1987 – see Table 2). In addition, since 1986, external
demand has been contributing negatively to GNP growth, whereas
domestic demand has been increasing steadily. Despite this change
Japan's GNP has grown at a rate of 4.2% in 1987 and 5.7% in 1988,
its highest level for fifteen years.

Table 2 Import of manufactured goods (1980–87)

Country	Share of total imports (%)			Amount (US$ million) 1987
	1980	1985	1987	
Japan	22.8	31.0	44.1	64,726
USA	56.8	76.5	79.6	299,552
Canada	74.8	84.5	85.6	74,627
West Germany	58.3	62.0	73.0	163,595
UK	67.2	70.6	76.8	117,163
France	57.7	62.0	73.9	114,372

Source: OECD, *Statistics of Foreign Trade*; MITI.

The effect on Japan's foreign economic policy brought about by the yen appreciation is considerable and cannot yet be completely understood. The changes, however, do integrate Japan more into the world economy through overseas investments and greater dependence on imported manufactured goods. This increases Japan's stake in other countries, for example, raising the need to protect overseas investments in manufacturing. The increase in national wealth is also attracting a growing number of Asian workers, who carry out menial jobs for which it has become difficult to find Japanese workers. This cannot fail to make Japan more conscious of its location and the plight of its Asian neighbours. The yen appreciation alone, however, will not solve Japan's trading problems: it will still have to open its markets and reorientate the export-driven nature of its economy. The volatility of exchange rates, as evidenced by the rise of the American dollar and subsequent decline of the yen since the beginning of 1989, emphasizes this point. Japan's surpluses with its major trading partners are still increasing, albeit at a lower rate, which demonstrates the resilience of the Japanese economy and its adaptability to the new currency exchange rates. The new pattern of more manufactured goods and fewer raw materials in the shares of imports produces mixed results for Japan's trading partners, which will have to adjust their markets. This particularly affects Third World countries, but also Australia and New Zealand.

Resource transfers to the Third World

The yen appreciation has also transformed Japan's position as an aid donor and given it the financial capability to greatly influence the Third World. Until the 1970s these regions, with the exception of the Asian countries, had remained rather distant from Japanese concerns. Apart from Brazil, a major destination for Japanese emigration during this century, the world outside Europe and North America did not matter much to the Japanese before the Pacific war, because it was under European rule. Even in Asia, Japan faced the European powers and the United States. After the war, through which it lost its empire in Asia, Japan was not involved in decolonization. In addition, Japan considered itself until recently a poor country, without a philanthropic tradition or, until the late 1970s, voluntary aid organizations.

This detachment changed during the 1970s as the first oil crisis of 1973 demonstrated to Japan the power of the Third World countries over those raw materials and energy resources on which it so crucially depended. Other developments, such as the growing instability of Third World countries and the Soviet invasion of Afghanistan, further stimulated Japan's interest in the Third World beyond East and Southeast Asia. Japan's political and economic leaders quickly learned the lesson. As shown in Chapter 5, Japan started to give 'strategic aid' to help those countries located in areas of strategic importance to the West. The need to develop more markets and broaden its supply basis of raw materials in order to avoid dependence on a few suppliers also prompted Japan's business sector to go into regions that it had so far neglected. As a result, for example, Japan has discovered Latin America, which provides essential raw materials and food supplies.

In 1960 Japan's ODA amounted to merely $105 million, and during the 1960s the country was itself the second largest beneficiary of World Bank funds, after India. By FY 1988, however, Japan's ODA topped that of all other aid donors, including the United

States, amounting to ¥1.35 trillion ($10 billion at an exchange rate of ¥135), a leap from $5.63 billion in 1986 and $7.45 billion in 1987. However, while the absolute amounts are large, the ratio of ODA to GNP is only 0.31%, much lower than the average of the members of the OECD's Development Assistance Committee (DAC). The quality of Japan's ODA remains low compared with other DAC countries: the bureaucratic structure for administering the growing funds is too weak and inefficient, and there are problems finding enough suitable projects. Japan's aid policies for the Third World are also hindered by factors extending beyond the usual problems of political instability or lack of capability to absorb aid. Japan's aid experience is still rather limited. Language and cultural unfamiliarity hinder most Japanese specialists travelling to these countries, while the aid recipients are reluctant to learn technical skills in Japan because of Japanese language requirements. The deep commitment of Japanese employees to their companies makes it very difficult to find people willing to go abroad for several years. As a result the proportion of technical aid in Japan's ODA is somewhat low.

About 65–70% of Japanese direct bilateral aid still goes to Asia, but Japan's past military and economic record in the region clouds the development of aid policy. There has been criticism that much of its aid is a thinly veiled subsidy for Japanese exports. Most of the aid so far has been for major investment projects such as infrastructures. The grant element is still relatively low, as most of the bilateral aid goes to Asian countries already receiving loans. Yen-denominated loans have also become unpopular with recipient countries because of the yen appreciation. In December 1987 in Manila Prime Minister Takeshita announced a $2 billion development fund to promote small and medium-sized businesses in the region. In 1986 the government announced its intention to channel $10 billion in worldwide ODA, mostly through multilateral aid agencies, and it added another $20 billion in 1987. However, the funds come from Japan's trade surplus and are mostly in the hands of the business sector, which of course, wants a good return and security; this means more loans at near-commercial rates. The difficulty which the government encounters in disbursing its aid is demonstrated by the fact that aid spending increased by no more than 3.4% annually between 1981 and 1986, whereas the aid budget itself rose by 9.8% a year.

In order to meet these criticisms the Japanese government has promised to spread its aid worldwide, to improve the grant element, and to increase the total amount. In June 1988 Tokyo announced its fourth 'doubling plan' for ODA since 1978 and promised to reach $50 billion during the period 1988–92, twice the amount disbursed in the 1983–7 period. Takeshita also announced his government's intention to raise the annual ODA figure to over $10 billion. Other measures include debt relief measures for the Least Developed Countries (LDCs), a $500 million aid package over a three-year period from 1987 to the LDCs of sub-Saharan Africa, and the intention to raise the GNP-ODA ratio from 0.31% to the DAC average of 0.35%. The Japanese government has been extremely skilful in maximizing publicity for these impressive figures; they have even appeared grandiose enough for Japan to be criticized for putting symbolism over substance. But the problem remains: how to realize these plans with an insufficient bureaucracy, tough conditions for the beneficiaries and a shortage of programmes which can absorb that much money quickly on the given conditions. Since Japan wants to avoid the creation of new debt problems for Third World countries and is willing to reduce their existing debt as a contribution to global stability, the government will have to further increase the share of grants and soften its conditions. Although Japan gives aid today to a total of 117 countries, more than any other donor, Asia will continue to receive the largest share.

7
TRILATERAL ECONOMIC INTERDEPENDENCE

The aftermath of the Pacific war brought Japan and the United States together in not only the close politico-security relationship described earlier, but also an economic relationship whose degree of integration is frequently overlooked by its proponents as well as by its critics. Just over 35% of Japan's exports go to the United States, but only about 20% of its imports have come from there in the past few years. Japan has become America's second largest export market after Canada, taking around 12% of US exports in 1987. Most of Japan's food imports come from the United States; this makes it the biggest market for US agricultural produce, with an annual import of around $7 billion. By March 1988, 38% of Japan's total cumulative FDI was in the United States, and, although still much less than British and Dutch investment in the United States, it has started to count in several industrial sectors such as the car industry and electronics. Communication links are also increasing by leaps and bounds; Japan is now the second largest market for overseas travel from the United States, surpassed only by Britain.

Because of the linkages and size of both economies, their economic relationship is of vital importance for the world economy and its management. Together, the two economies account for about one-third of total world GNP. If something goes wrong in their relationship, it will directly affect other countries. For instance, when the United States limited Japanese car imports, Japanese car makers attempted to sell more on the European market. The outcome of current trade conflicts will weigh heavily on the final US stance on protectionism. Yet the degree of cooperation, as opposed to competition, between both economies will determine the degree of autonomy and scope for development of economic relations with other countries or regions such as Western Europe and Asia. The rhetoric of the Euro-Japanese economic relationship suggests many similarities with Japan-US relations, but the scope of trade and investment and consequent interdependence and entwinement is still, despite recent growth, far less significant.

Trade

The United States

The major trading partner of Japan since 1945 has always been the United States. Until the second half of the 1960s, the difference in size between the two economies was so great that Japan could pursue its economic rehabilitation and the expansion into the world market without major clashes of interest. At the end of the 1960s, however, textile exports to the United States became a major issue and Japan had to conclude the first in a long series of self-restraint agreements. These have grown in number, through sectors such as automobiles in 1981 to semiconductors in 1986. In the 1970s and 1980s, the number of trade conflicts and their intensity steadily increased, involving a wide range of items such as textiles, steel, automobiles, tobacco, agricultural products, machine tools and semiconductors.

The worsening bilateral economic relationship has to be seen against the background of a general deterioration of US competitiveness on the world market. The US trade balance sank from a surplus of $5 billion in 1960 to a deficit of $171 billion in 1987. In manufactured goods it slipped from a surplus of $11 billion in 1981 to a deficit of $32 billion in 1985, reflecting a 32% decrease by volume in manufacturing exports during the same period.

Several factors exacerbated the situation. First, although the Japanese market is opening fast to the outside, and tariff barriers as well as quantitative restrictions are either very low or fewer than in other industrialized countries, there still exists a range of non-tariff barriers to trade, such as the expensive and complicated distribution system and difficult access to public procurement. The case of foreign participation in the bidding for the construction of Kansai airport in 1988–9 illustrated the latter point. Second, some trade obstacles result from different social and political mores; these problems have often been aggravated by US marketing failures and indifference to foreign trade.[7] Third, the increasing technological sophistication of Japanese production raises fears amongst those in the United States who want to protect the US superiority over the Soviet Union in weapon technology. When it became known in 1987 that the Toshiba Machine Corporation had sold the Soviet Union machine tools which could be used for the production of submarine screws, many Americans considered it a serious security breach by Japan, and the scandal temporarily linked conflicts in the economic relationship with those in the security relationship. Fourth, the US trade balance is negative not only with Japan, but also with the Asian NICs, which have dramatically increased their exports of manufactured goods to the United States. Finally, the differences in the political system of both countries make it difficult to resolve trade problems outside the public limelight. The US political system is much more open for specific interests to win influence far beyond their relative importance in the national economy. Differing negotiating styles add to the problem. Since the mid-1980s the US approach to opening the Japanese market has been through market-orientated, sector-selective (MOSS) negotiations, which target a certain sector and focus considerable attention on it for a sustained period. Japanese reactions are seen as slow and foot-dragging. As a result, tensions reached a new climax in 1987 when President Reagan, in order to avoid even harsher Congress action, imposed a $300 million tariff on certain Japanese electronics imports.

The Omnibus Trade Act, which was finally passed by the US Congress in August 1988, could become a new watershed in Japanese-US trade relations. Under the clause which has become popularly known as 'Super 301', the US president can take retaliatory action against countries which are deemed to engage in unfair trade practices. It will depend on the president how he will use the increased powers against trading partners in order to force countries with trade surpluses, like Japan, on to what is called a 'level field'. The climate in the United States towards Japan has hardened again since the start of the Bush administration and there are strong voices in support of using the Trade Act against Japan and the NIEs. Faced with the limited results achieved in sectoral market-opening negotiations, there is growing support in the United States for managed trade, which will require the Japanese to reserve for US exporters a certain market share in selected Japanese sectors. At the same time, economic integration has developed to such an extent that drastic action would probably hurt certain US industrial sectors more than those of the Japanese. Major US industrial corporations actually cooperated with Japanese lobbyists to tone down the trade bill in 1988 in order to avoid a repetition of the damage incurred after the semiconductor agreement.

A more long-term US approach to solving the trade problem is the idea of a Free Trade Agreement (FTA), which gained some momentum towards the end of the Reagan administration. The underlying philosophy is that free, unhindered trade will sort out all bilateral economic frictions. In 1984 the US Special Trade Representative, William Brock, proposed talks to ASEAN member countries for a United States-ASEAN FTA. In April 1985 a US-Israeli FTA was signed and in May 1988 a similar agreement was signed with Canada. In January 1988 Reagan proposed a US-Japanese FTA to Prime Minister Takeshita, who instructed MITI and the Foreign Ministry to work out a feasibility study. The realization of an FTA with Japan seems extremely unlikely in the face of rising protectionism in the United States and the weakened US economic position, which would make Japan the major beneficiary of unrestricted access to the US market. It is not clear whether this idea has after all been floated only as a political counter to suspicions of West European intentions to build a protectionist EC bloc.

Although the election of another Republican president, George Bush, guaranteed some continuity in US approaches to trade with Japan, the voices demanding managed trade are becoming stronger as the economic difficulties of the United States and its trade deficit

Table 3 Japan's main trading partners, 1987

Trading partner	Exports (US$ million)	Share in total exports (%)	Imports (US$ million)	Share in total imports (%)
USA	83,580	36.5	31,490	21.1
EC	37,693	16.4	17,670	11.8
S. Korea	13,229	5.8	8,075	5.4
W. Germany	12,833	5.6	6,150	4.1
Taiwan	11,346	4.9	7,128	4.8
China	8,250	3.6	7,401	5.0
Australia	5,146	2.2	7,869	5.3
Canada	5,611	2.4	6,073	4.1
UK	8,400	3.7	3,057	2.0

Source: Japan 1989: An International Comparison, Keizai Koho Center, Tokyo.

with the world grow. Hammering at sensitive sectors like agriculture, notably for the liberalization of Japanese rice imports, may heighten tensions. The failure to achieve a compromise on agricultural subsidies within the Uruguay round of the GATT is an indication of the growing US impatience with its trading partners.

The European Community
Japan's trade with the EC is less than half that with the United States; according to Japanese statistics, total trade with the EC amounted in 1987 to $55 billion, compared to $115 billion with the United States (see Table 3). Thanks to increased domestic demand in Japan, the EC could actually reduce its deficit in 1987 for the first time in nine years, by 3% to 21 billion ECUs, although in dollar terms, the European deficit rose from $16 billion to $20 billion, following the depreciation of the dollar vis-à-vis the yen. Most of this trade deficit is with West Germany. In 1987, European exports to Japan increased by 19%, but Japanese exports to the EC still rose by 6.1% (while they fell by 5.6% to the rest of the world and by 10.4% to the United States).[8] Moreover it is doubtful whether Japan will continue to reduce its deficit with the EC.

Like the United States, the EC continues to press for further market opening. In 1985 the EC Commission started to demand from Japan 'quantified import targets' in order to reach a 'balance of benefits', while at the same time working for better access to certain market sectors in Japan. These import targets were opposed by Japan because they would lead to a managed trading system. The EC has also resorted to bringing cases before the GATT, and in several instances, such as over liquor taxes and the Japan-US semiconductor agreement, it has been successful.

In order to stem the flood of imports from Japan the EC has recently strengthened its instruments for controlling Japanese trade. What began in 1981 with the surveillance of the most contentious products, such as cars, colour TVs and machine tools, has now been augmented by Commission powers so that punitive duties can be imposed on goods which are found to be sold at dumping prices. In one case the dubious character of such punitive duties was demonstrated in the summer of 1988, when Japanese dot-matrix printers were subjected to a duty of up to 34% because of alleged dumping. Yet Japan already virtually monopolizes this market sector and there is no European market share in this category to warrant protection. In the end, it is the European customer who suffers. For its part, Japan is negotiating with the EC Commission on the elimination of European import quotas on 106 items considered by Japan to be targeted especially against itself. At present about half of Japan's trade with the EC is subject to some kind of restriction, and the government is concerned about the handling of this quota system under the new conditions which will prevail in the unified EC market after 1992.

Investment

Although the increased FDI is received somewhat ambivalently in the United States and the EC, this outflow will very soon fundamentally change the nature of Japan's external economic relations and thus exert great influence on Japan's foreign policy as well. It will alter the structure of Japan's economy and increase its political stake in the stability of other countries.

The United States

The effect of Japanese FDI on economic relations with the United

States is particularly marked, because that is where most of Japan's FDI is directed. The two driving forces for increased investment there are the size and importance of the US market, which is threatened by protectionist actions, and the appreciation of the yen, particularly against the dollar. Over the last decade, Japan has invested more in the United States than in Southeast Asia, which was formerly the prime target. At the end of FY 1987, the total stock value of Japanese FDI in the United States amounted to $50.2 billion (see Table 4). This represented 36% of total Japanese FDI (Britain and the Netherlands are still bigger investors in stock values). In 1987 alone Japanese investment in real estate in the United States went up by 86% to a total of $13 billion. During 1988 British investors committed $32.5 billion to acquire 400 American companies, whereas Japanese commitments were estimated for the same period at $12 billion.[9] In 1988 about 160,000 Americans in the manufacturing sector were employed by wholly- or partly-owned Japanese ventures. Forty US states have offices in Tokyo trying, through a variety of incentives, to lure even more Japanese investments. About 50% of the Japanese investment in 1987 was in wholesale and retail trade, 16% in manufacturing and banking/finance, and 13% in real estate.

Politically, the most sensitive areas for Japanese FDI are manufacturing and real estate. The latter is less important in economic terms but highly visible, and therefore attracts considerable public attention. In manufacturing, Japanese companies have concentrated on those industries which are most threatened by protectionism, notably cars. As a result, rising Japanese investment in its own car production plants or other joint ventures with US car companies have led to exports to the United States shrinking since FY 1987 to levels even below the limit of 2.3 million allowed by the car self-restraint agreement. A rising number of Japanese companies in the United States now find it profitable to export their goods to Japan, because of higher production costs back in Japan. More Japanese companies will become dependent on the profitability of their operations in the United States or other countries, thus increasing their stake in the prosperity of the US economy and enhancing the integration of both economies. This tendency does, however, feed into the debate within Japan about the 'hollowing out' of the Japanese production base by the removal overseas of vital industrial production. Some argue that this is weakening Japan in the medium term, while others argue that Japan has to concentrate on higher added-value products and services in order to survive.

Although foreign-owned firms' control of assets represented only 9% of total non-financial corporate assets in the United States in 1986 – and the Japanese share was still very small – there has been some concern about the domination of certain sectors by Japan. It hurts American pride to realize that the manufacturing costs of certain products, like cars and TV sets, are now lower in their own country than in Japan, the reverse of the situation they were used to previously in relationships with developing countries. It is also uncertain whether these Japanese investments are actually contributing to the production potential of the United States or are only displacing the indigenous industry.

The rising stake of Japan in the US economy is especially visible in its investments in the financial market. Japan became the biggest single buyer of US Treasury bonds, thereby, in effect, financing the Reagan administration's policy of tax cuts and tremendous increases in military expenditure. The Japanese financial market is still comparatively limited and the US market offers the opportunity to place the huge sums of money accrued from its trade surplus. The Japanese government has encouraged this capital flow, because it forestalled potentially serious implications for Japan's most important economic and security partner. But owing to the continued instability of the dollar, the profit margin for Japanese bond purchases declines when the dollar falls, and there is a gradual reorientation towards other markets, notably Europe. For these reasons the Japanese government has in the last few years strongly supported the dollar. A breakthrough in the situation can happen only if the United States can restore the economy and confidence in the dollar. It is also intriguing to consider that US demands for greater Japanese domestic consumption and liberalization would

Table 4 Japan's direct overseas investment (as of 31 March 1988)

Region/country	No. of cases	Cumulative amount (US$ million)
North America, total	16,408	52,763
Europe, total	4,861	21,047
UK	1,368	6,598
Luxembourg	117	4,072
Netherlands	425	3,166
West Germany	867	1,955
France	841	1,300
Switzerland	242	977
Spain	187	883
Asia, total	13,691	26,658
South America, total	5,930	25,189
World total	44,707	139,334

Source: *Japan 1989: An International Comparison*, Keizai Koho Center, Tokyo.

actually contribute to a further reduction in the amount of Japanese money available for US government bonds.

The European Community
Japanese FDI in the EC has also been increasing, if anything more dramatically since 1986 than into the United States. In Western Europe it increased during FY 1987 by an astonishing 90% over the previous year. Europe's share of total investment abroad in 1987 by Japanese companies rose from 15% to almost 20%. Although cumulative FDI amounted to only $21 billion at the end of FY 1987 (see Table 4), it had reached $30.2 billion a year later. In the United Kingdom alone, Japanese FDI rose two-and-a-half times, to reach $2.47 billion during 1987. Japanese manufacturing outlets in Britain now number around 86 and employed, as of autumn 1988, at least 21,000 people. However, according to a survey, at the beginning of 1987 the 220 Japanese companies operating in the EC employed 75,000 people, less than IBM alone.[10]

As in the United States, Japanese investment in the EC has not been without its problems. Japan's production assets there are less significant than in the United States, while their share in total production is also lower. It is possible that what is now a convenient solution to a short-term problem may create in the future even greater long-term problems. Japanese investment in manufacturing may become politically untenable because European investment in Japan is so much lower. While trade deficits can be reduced by draconian measures (e.g. voluntary export restrictions), Japanese factories cannot simply be closed by the host governments, because of investment and employment protection arrangements. Japanese manufacturing investment is often seen as helpful for employment in depressed regions, particularly in the case of the United Kingdom. The EC tries to counter the danger of simple assembly operations ('screwdriver operations') by trying to find a consensus for a European content ratio. A Japanese survey at the beginning of 1988 had put the average European content ratio of Japanese companies in Europe at 44%. In 1987 a new Community law was enacted which extended anti-dumping duties for imports to products assembled inside the EC using a high proportion of dumped components from Japan. It was first applied, in 1988, to four Japanese-owned electronic typewriter firms based in the United Kingdom and France. The problem here is that in some cases the Japanese may find it difficult to conform, because of local sourcing problems; in order to reach the ceiling they may opt for simpler designs needing fewer Japanese components (such a case has been reported for copying machines). This will not only reduce one of the benefits of Japanese investment in Europe – the influx of new technology – but also treat Europeans as second-class customers. Recently the technological sophistication of Japanese investment has been increasing and some Japanese companies are even establishing research laboratories within the EC to tap into the European technological potential.

Japanese investment has also created intra-EC tensions as other member countries occasionally do not recognize locally manufactured goods as European because of the Japanese content. For example, cars produced by Nissan in Sunderland (UK) were not given the status of EC products because French local content regulations did not allow foreign companies a transitory period for gearing up to 80%, as the British government does. Only after strong British pressure did the French give way. Other disputes revolve around the extent of the subsidies given by individual EC countries to Japanese investors. The basic problem is, of course, the lack of a common EC policy on foreign investment and local content.

High technology

Nowhere is the issue of interdependence and integration of the US and Japanese economies clearer than in the high-technology sector. More than anything else, the handling of high-technology issues will affect the sustainability and future direction of the relationship as a whole. The United States has become very concerned about Japan's advances in this field, in what is perceived as a one-way street in technological exchange. The situation is compounded by different perceptions of the links between national security and technology, by the instrumentalization of technological transfers in East-West relations, and by different industrial structures. Japan has no military-industrial complex like that in the United States, where there is a significant impact on the civilian sector of US industry in terms of research foci, finances and labour. Until the Toshiba scandal in 1987, indeed, national security considerations were virtually absent from Japan's approach to technology. Japan has greatly expanded its position in the bilateral high-technology trade. Japanese competition is keenly felt in several areas relevant to basic industrial competitiveness, and thus to US military preparedness, such as electronics, where Japan has supplemented the United States in innovative applications, new materials and production technology.

Semiconductors, the 'raw material' of the new industrial age, were singled out by US producers who accused Japanese industry of unfair trade practices. In order to preclude even harsher congressional action, in September 1986 the Reagan administration concluded a highly-contested semiconductor agreement with Japan to end the dumping of Japanese-manufactured semiconductors in the United States and third markets and to achieve better US access to the Japanese market. However, the agreement has come to epitomize the failure of such administrative intrusions. Not only did it not solve the US grievances, it actually hurt US industry. Japanese producers, as required by the agreement, raised their prices, reaping enormous windfall profits and wounding manufacturers around the world, especially computer makers, who rely heavily on Japanese semiconductors. European industry was also hurt, and a GATT panel, established after a complaint by the EC Commission, ruled that the Japanese price-monitoring system set up under the bilateral agreement violated the rules of the GATT.

The rise in takeovers of US companies, Japanese investment in US production facilities and the financing of R&D activities in the United States by major Japanese corporations have only compounded the problem of high technology. Measures have even been taken to prevent Japanese takeovers of US companies which produce equipment deemed to be sensitive to national security, and to limit the free flow of civilian high-technology information. One notable case occurred in 1986 with the planned partial takeover of the French-owned company Fairchild Semiconductors, one of the foremost microchip makers in the United States, by Fujitsu, a leading Japanese electronics company. Fairchild is a major supplier of chips to US military contractors, and, under pressure from the Department of Defense, Fujitsu in the end renounced the acquisition of a share majority.

In the civilian sector, the Reagan administration tried to encourage the international flow of high technology worldwide and at the same time to secure a better protection of intellectual property rights. After two-and-a-half years of difficult negotiation, both countries signed a revised Science and Technology Agreement in June 1988. This agreement has become a symbol of their increasingly divergent ideas on technology policy. The Japanese were not interested in a revision of the original 1980 agreement; but the United States was, because it wanted to increase research cooperation, create a 'more equal balance', change what it calls the 'one-way flow of exchange', and obtain 'symmetrical access' to Japanese research facilities. The greatest obstacles to the conclusion of a new agreement concerned the proprietary rights relating to the results of joint research and the handling of the security aspects of such results. Accordingly, under the new agreement, the country in which the results of the joint research were obtained owns the proprietary rights and can decide on the transfer of these rights to third countries. Demands by the United States for changes to the rules governing transfers to third countries, in the case of militarily relevant results, led to an impasse in the negotiating of the agreement. Moreover, the United States wished Japan to revise its patent systems along the lines of the US patent system, which would also present problems for the EC. The Omnibus Trade Act of August 1988 also increased the presidential power to protect the proprietary rights of US industry.

Europe also understands that it risks being excluded from Japanese high technology if it leaves Japan to the United States and the Pacific rim. Since Japan is concerned not to miss out on some technological development arising from European joint research programmes like ESPRIT or EUREKA, high technology has become a focus for Japanese-European cooperation. In April 1988 the groundwork was laid in Osaka for a joint research centre, aimed at promoting technological exchange between Japan and Europe.

Japan and the United States: how close is too close?
Within the past decade, the economic interdependence and integration of the United States and Japan have come to parallel their already close security relationship. However, as the relationship becomes more interlinked and intimate, matters of great national sensitivity become involved. For example, high technology becomes linked to competitiveness, national security or the predominance in a sector of the economy of the other side. These issues are on the increase and they are much more intractable than earlier trade disputes over textiles and citrus fruit quotas.

A fundamental problem with the invocation of national security by the United States is its lack of definition. Its indiscriminate use sometimes appears intentional, particularly when it is to the advantage of commercial interests. The key words are 'dependence' or 'dependency', which are seldom clearly defined. Instead, 'dependence' is at once associated with 'vulnerability'. The question of what leverage is given to the other side in a situation of dependence has barely been examined. Is it likely that the Japanese would have an interest in depriving the United States of their products? Is there not an equal interest on the selling side? The absence of real leverage is best illustrated by the Japanese purchase of US Treasury bonds, which thereby financed a quarter to a third of the US deficit. If Japan suddenly demanded cash for these bonds the United States would be in great difficulties. However, this situation does not translate into much leverage for the Japanese, since they are dependent on the United States as a supplier of markets, raw materials, foodstuffs and a security guarantee, as well as a financial market in which to invest their funds generated from trade surpluses.

The issue of dependence raises the fundamental question of the degree of trust the United States is able and willing to put in Japan. Does the United States view Japan as a reliable ally under all conditions or just as a useful ally during good times? The increasingly closely interwoven military relationship looks most endangered when viewed in conjunction with economic and security matters, as was the case particularly under the Reagan administration. A report by the Defense Department's Defense Science Board in February 1987 urged less dependence on Japan in electronics by arguing that 'while Japan is a strong and essential ally, its economic interests occasionally differ from those of the United States'.[11]

The question asked is whether the Japanese competitor would give his best to a foreigner or hold back to preserve a competitive advantage. Rather than as a useful ally, Japan is increasingly seen as a threat to the economic welfare of the United States and is spoken of in terms previously reserved for the 'Soviet threat'. Some even portray it as the more immediate threat.[12] The COCOM violation by Toshiba only heightened this perception and directly linked Japan to the 'Soviet threat'.

Inevitably, intensifying conflicts in the economic relationship provoke the question of how long the Japanese-US relationship can survive without suffering long-term damage and in particular whether these conflicts will start to undermine the security relationship. The level of tension has risen since the 1970s, but, paradoxically, so has the degree of cooperation and integration. So far the balance between the growth of conflict and the growth of cooperation in the economic field has been maintained. The main reason is, of course, that no side could leave the other without suffering unacceptable damage. Japan cannot do without the US security guarantee and market, and the United States needs Japan to maintain its global role and to bolster its fading economic and technological strength. Yet reliance on Japanese strength involves not only abandoning certain great-power privileges and interests, but also granting Japan a bigger say in international affairs. This means a proportional reduction of US as well as European influence over world affairs. Such a transfer of power and influence would be at best extremely delicate; it is all the more difficult for a superpower like the United States, which, because of its size, enjoys so much residual power and so many natural advantages.

Japan and Europe: towards a better economic relationship
Although economic frictions are far from levelling off, Japan and Western Europe are discovering that a more positive and constructive economic relationship must be built up. This has been helped by an increase in European exports to Japan – in the case of Britain a rise of 26% in 1987 over 1986 – owing to the expansion of domestic consumption in Japan. Advances have been made in further opening up the Japanese market for products the EC is most interested in. Increasingly, this includes the financial market (access to the Tokyo Stock Exchange) and the market in services. As a result relations became less acrimonious in 1988, though they have yet to be given more substance and continuity. Japan recognizes the usefulness of Western Europe in the joint management of the world economy and the management of a close but troubled Japanese-US relationship. Japan's political and economic leaders realize also that they need European support against the growing protectionist temptations in the United States. The debt crisis of the Third World is another issue where dialogue between Japan and the EC has increased. Japan looks also for European advice in carrying out its pledge to recycle $30 billion to the Third World; during his two European visits in 1988, Takeshita consulted with European countries on how to spend the $500 million in grant aid which his government wanted to give to sub-Saharan Africa during the next three years. In some cases

British Crown Agents are actually handling the disbursement for the Japanese government.

Although the West European market is already quite substantial, nothing has galvanized Japanese attention more than the prospect of a unified EC market by 1992, which would boost growth and competitiveness by freeing up trade and capital movement within the Community. The Japanese are both mystified and alarmed by contradictory statements from their European partners, at one time stressing that the single market would certainly not eliminate all trade restrictions merely so as to erect new ones for outsiders, and at another emphasizing that outsiders have to offer something in return in order to enjoy the openness of the future unified market.

The European Community, for its part, is concerned that Japan is developing a special relationship with the United States which threatens to jeopardize its interests. The granting of preferential conditions to US business, such as the opening of the construction market in 1988, is viewed with suspicion. Even though the decline of the dollar has benefited the United States rather than the EC, there are fears in Japan about the United States and Europe ganging up against Japan. This has not happened so far, as the United States has felt strong enough to extract concessions from Japan on its own, a feeling nurtured by successes in the opening of the construction and beef markets. Thus at economic summit meetings or in the preparation of the latest GATT round, for example, the Reagan administration resisted the inclusion of clauses directed against Japan.

In sum, the Japanese-European economic relationship faces similar challenges to the Japanese-US one, albeit on a smaller scale. No way has yet been found to effectively diminish the Japanese trade surplus, and the remedy of increased Japanese FDI in Europe may only create an imbalance which is even more difficult to redress. At the same time, however, economic interdependence between Japan and Europe is growing, both in the reciprocal relationship and in the management of the world economy. Moreover, compared to the US attitude to its economic relationship with Japan, there is much greater willingness in Europe to tackle problems in a constructive way.

8
THE ASIAN-PACIFIC ECONOMIC BLOC

When Dean Acheson wrote in 1947 that Japan's economy must be reconstructed because the recovery of Asia depended on it, few could have anticipated the success of this idea. As the United States, for political reasons, did not want Japan to re-enter the Chinese market, Japan had to focus its attention on Southeast Asia. In the middle of the 1960s Japan relaxed its foreign-currency controls, allowing medium-sized companies to set up plants in Southeast Asia in order to profit from low labour costs, while the general trading houses started to invest in the extraction of raw materials and energy resources of the region. When Japan started to provide development aid, Asia naturally became the prime recipient since it had helped Japan to develop its markets and its resources.

Over the succeeding two decades, the region stretching from Burma to Japan has become more diversified both in its political structure and in terms of economic performance. A 'three-stage' economic hierarchy has emerged, which in practice tends to resemble the 'flying geese' pattern of development much beloved by Japanese economists. Japan is at the top providing aid, investment funds, technology and, increasingly, market opportunities for the products of the region. Next are the NIEs, consisting of South Korea, Taiwan, Hong Kong and Singapore. These countries are at the developmental stage that Japan was at in the 1960s and depend on Japan for investment, technology, spare parts and markets. The

NIEs are followed by the other member states of ASEAN, notably Thailand and Malaysia, and by China. Because of the dynamism of development at all these levels and the growing linkages between them in terms of trade and investment, each country is forced to improve continually and upgrade its industrial structure and performance.

Almost absent from the economic development and entwinement of the region is the Soviet Union. In the 1960s and 1970s there were great expectations in Japan about the exploitation of resources in the Asian part of the Soviet Union. However, Soviet pre-conditions, the cooling of East-West relations and falling raw material prices interrupted this development. As he spelled out in his speeches at Vladivostok in July 1986 and Krasnoyarsk in September 1988, Gorbachev is determined that the Soviet Union should tap into the economic dynamism of the Asian Pacific. Since January 1987 the Soviet Union has allowed joint ventures, under which the foreign partner could have a maximum share of 49%. This was increased to 99% in December 1988, but the Japanese have been very cautious. By the end of June 1989 only 18 agreements on Soviet joint ventures had been signed by Japanese companies, compared with 97 negotiated by West German and 48 by British companies. The Soviet Union, however, considers Japan the key to the booming Pacific region and is eager to obtain Japanese technology. The prospects are rather dim, because the Japanese government tries to link political issues – the return of the Northern Territories – to the conclusion of a long-term trade agreement, while Japanese business arrives at the same outcome by judging its commitments on the basis of profitability. However, increasing trade, and even investment, linking other East Asian countries, such as South Korea, with the Soviet Union will exert some pressure on Japan to do likewise.

The NIEs

The change in Japan's economic relationship with Asia is most visible with the NIEs. Until recently Japan invested in these countries primarily because of the labour cost differentials, and the products were mostly exported to the United States. The share of the

NIEs in total US imports grew from 6.4% ($19.2 billion) in 1980 to around 12% or $87.2 billion in 1987. For all four NIEs, the United States has taken over 25% of their total exports throughout the mid-1980s. Thus the United States has been the most important facilitator of the economic development of the NIEs. But at the same time, the United States has accumulated trade deficits with the NIEs which surpass its trade deficit with the EC. By contrast, Japan's trade surpluses with the NIEs have steadily grown through the 1980s, peaking in 1987.

Since 1985 the appreciation of the yen and increasing domestic costs have forced Japanese companies to invest more in the NIEs; in dollar terms FY 1986 saw increases in FDI of 22.5% to South Korea and 155% to Taiwan. As a result Japan had also to import more from the four NIEs: their share grew from 5.3% ($7.4 billion) in 1980 to 11.8% in the first half of 1987. Overall trade between Japan and the NIEs increased from $3.2 billion in 1970 to $58.8 billion in 1987 (in the latter year almost exactly equal to Japan-EC trade). Japan is thus taking over some of the functions of the US market for the NIEs. Although manufactured products from the NIEs, as well as other Asian countries, are still considered inferior in quality in Japan, consumers are gradually changing their attitudes in the face of cheaper prices and improving quality. There are now even some chain-stores which specialize in the sale of products from the NIEs.

Japan is actually being forced through a combination of the rising yen, increasing labour costs at home and the growing industrial sophistication of the NIEs to leave an increasing amount of medium-technology production to the NIEs. Since many of their manufacturing plants are either Japanese subsidiaries or depend on Japanese parts, however, Japan's exports to the NIEs have also been increasing dramatically: from $19.2 billion in 1980 to $37 billion in 1987. But the share of the NIEs in total Japanese exports grew only from 14.8% to 16.9% over the same period.[13] While these new manufactures in the NIEs displace Japan's indigenous production of medium-level technology products like TV sets, VTRs and microwave ovens, they also help Japan to move into higher-technology products. This helps to reduce the weight of its own dual economy and enables it to continue to sell consumer electronics to the United States through its Asian subsidiaries, without incurring direct political costs. The transition is not easy for Japan and, ironically, it finds itself now in a similar situation to that experienced earlier by the United States and Western Europe, when they were forced to leave certain industrial sectors because of Japanese dominance. In 1987, for the first time this century, Japan became a net importer of textiles, and the Japanese government even considered in 1988–9 imposing dumping charges on South Korea, which eventually agreed, however, to an export restraint agreement.

The next few years will not be easy ones for the relationship between Japan and the NIEs, but the continuing prosperity of this group of countries depends on Japan opening its markets faster to their exports. The US trade deficit with many Asian countries encourages tendencies to close the US market, a move which will ultimately have negative implications for Japan's direct exports to the United States and Europe. Tensions will further rise because the NIEs had their benefits under the Generalized System of Preferences (GSP) removed by the United States at the beginning of 1989. For this reason, and in order not to hinder their economic development at a critical juncture, Japan continues to apply the GSP. Although the EC is also increasing its trade with the NIEs, Japan, as the major provider of investment and technology, will play a more significant role in preventing an economic recession in their economies.

ASEAN and Indochina

Relations with the resource-rich Southeast Asian countries regained their prewar importance in the mid-1970s, after the first oil shock and the traumatic demonstrations against Prime Minister Tanaka Kakuei, who visited the region in 1974. Although these student demonstrators used the occasion of Tanaka's visit partially to vent their dissatisfaction with domestic politics, they did have a considerable effect on Japanese perceptions of the region. Japan realized that its hegemonic position as a prime source for FDI and as a trading partner had to be addressed. In 1975 the postwar reparation agreements ended with a call for the redefinition of economic cooperation between Japan and Asia. In addition, the United States pressed Japan to shoulder more responsibilities for economic development and regional stability after its own withdrawal from Vietnam in 1975. Against this background, Prime Minister Fukuda Takeo enunciated in August 1977 his so-called 'Fukuda doctrine', which promised to pay greater attention to ASEAN.

However, his policy did not come over well. Japan's strong involvement in economic assistance to China was seen not only as making ASEAN appear secondary, but also as supporting a great power which was still considered by several ASEAN countries to be a greater threat than the Soviet Union or its Vietnamese ally. This view applied particularly to Indonesia. At first the Japanese government had set a kind of unofficial ceiling on aid to China, which meant that aid to Indonesia was to be higher in absolute terms. This was then abandoned in favour of more economic assistance to China. Japan was also unjustifiably blamed for the demise of five major ASEAN industrial projects which never fully materialized because of the failing consensus among the ASEAN countries. Japan had promised massive assistance but, faced with ASEAN's failure, only money for feasibility studies resulted.

Political considerations for aid to ASEAN increased, first after the US withdrawal from Indochina in 1975, and then after Vietnam's invasion of Kampuchea. Recognizing the value of ASEAN as a regional group for strengthening the countries of Southeast Asia, Japan calibrated its position on the Indochina issue throughout the 1980s as a way of enhancing ASEAN. In July 1987 Japan declared that it would add credibility to ASEAN's position on Kampuchea, which it had consistently supported, by contributing to peace-keeping operations, and by furnishing humanitarian and economic assistance to all three Indochinese countries after the settlement of the situation in Kampuchea. Nevertheless, much to the resentment of the ASEAN countries, Japan-Vietnam trade rose to ¥50 billion in 1985, making Japan Vietnam's biggest trading partner after the Soviet Union.

Within the ASEAN group, the Philippines has been receiving particular attention since Cory Aquino's government came to power in 1986. Japan is the country's top creditor, and although it is willing to step up economic assistance in order to prop up the Aquino government and provide a good environment for the US-Philippine talks on the future of the US bases, the limited absorption capability of the country as well as the past record of Japanese involvement in corruption during the Marcos era hamper these intentions.

Japanese ODA is still concentrated on Asia, and six countries actually receive more than half of Japan's total aid worldwide; China, Thailand and Indonesia are the major recipients now. Japan is also the most important supplier of economic assistance to several industrial countries: Thailand receives 68% of its aid from Japan, the Philippines 56% and Malaysia 55%. In December 1987 Prime Minister Takeshita made his first foreign visit, to Manila, in order to attend the third ASEAN summit meeting. He promised financial cooperation of no less than $2 billion over a period of three years, consisting of both investments and loans. Until the mid-1980s Japanese investment in ASEAN was declining in absolute terms. However, the appreciation of the yen and the increased competitiveness of the NIEs has encouraged Japan increasingly to direct investments into the rest of ASEAN, notably Thailand and Malaysia, as well as into China. Japan is now the largest source of FDI flows to Indonesia, Malaysia and Thailand. With this increased Japanese investment more technology is flowing into the region, a response to one of the central requests of ASEAN to Japan.

China

When Japan normalized relations with China in 1972, expectations on both sides concerning the expansion of the economic relationship were very high. Japan has always wanted to go back to the Chinese continent but was prevented from tapping China's internal market and raw materials by the anti-communist China stance of its US ally. Until 1972 only modest trade relations were possible; these were skilfully used by China to reach its political goals, such as the normalization of relations and the denting of the Western anti-communist China front. At the same time Japan attempted to protect its fiction of a separation between politics and economics.

In the second half of the 1980s Japan became, after Hong Kong, China's second largest trading partner and its largest lender.

However, the trade relationship has had its difficulties: over cancellations of Chinese plant orders in 1979–80 because of a change in China's external trade policy; over curtailment of Chinese oil deliveries (the most important Chinese export item to Japan) at the beginning of the 1980s, when Chinese domestic consumption increased rapidly; over Japan's bilateral trade surplus in every year since 1972 except 1981 and 1983; and over the delivery of faulty products from Japan in the 1980s. Total trade increased from $1.1 billion in 1972 to a peak of $18.7 billion in 1985. In 1986, out of a total of 1,691 business representative offices in China, 564 were Japanese and 203 were American. Because China wanted to reduce its overall trade deficit with its Western partners, notably Japan, trade fell to a level of $15.6 billion in 1987. The Japanese surplus was thus reduced from $5.13 billion in 1985 to $1.32 billion in 1987. Trade has been Japan's most important tool so far in gaining a strong foothold in China. Although China is now trying to reduce this dependence on Japan, it will be impossible, for example, for European enterprises to rival the Japanese position and market penetration efforts.

Japanese FDI is an area with great long-term growth potential in China. From 1979 to 1987 there were only 395 cases of Sino-Japanese joint ventures; in FY 1986 the cumulative Japanese FDI total of $600 million in China amounted to only 0.5% of total Japanese FDI, compared to nearly twice as much Japanese investment in Taiwan. In cumulative terms Japan trails behind the investments of the overseas Chinese and the United States. The Japanese business sector has concluded that at the heart of the problem are the lack of legal guarantees, stringent Chinese conditions which encourage exports but which keep foreigners out of the huge internal Chinese market, and the underdevelopment of the industrial infrastructure. For the production of parts or assembly jobs, the Southeast Asian nations are much more profitable because conditions are easier and labour is one-third of the cost in China. However, at least until June 1989 Japanese FDI in China was increasing rapidly, partly because of the investment protection agreement concluded in August 1988 after more than seven years of negotiation, and partly because of Japan's need for foreign production bases. With production costs increasing in South Korea and

Taiwan, and manufacturers of these countries starting to move their own production facilities to China as political relations ease, Japan is being forced into increasing its investment for competitive reasons. Another incentive for further investment in China is the relaxing of rules concerning joint ventures and the acceptance of 100% foreign-owned ventures. Japan has been for several years China's largest provider of loans, most of which are allocated to major projects. It has extended a five-year yen loan of ¥300 billion, beginning in FY 1979 after the economic opening-up of China, and a seven-year loan of ¥470 billion, beginning in FY 1984. This was topped in 1988 by a third yen loan of ¥600 billion over six years from FY 1990. Since 1982 China has been the single biggest recipient of Japanese aid.

These aid, trade and investment developments, coming on top of geographic contiguity and economic complementarity, have enlarged the foundation of Japan's relationship with China. As long as economic frictions can be limited, the economic platform provides a cushion against frictions in the political realm, while helping China to build an economic foundation for political stability. So far, while relations with China have been integrated into Japan's regionalist policies, these relations have not interfered with Japan's links with the rest of Asia. The more quickly China becomes committed to the 'three-stage' development model outlined earlier in terms of regional economic integration, the better it will be for regional stability and for smooth Sino-Japanese relations.

Interdependence in the Asian-Pacific region

The 'three-stage' scale of dynamic economic development in the Asian-Pacific region has led to a growing economic interdependence. The rapid and varied development of the countries of this region in the 1980s, as raw material sources, manufacturing bases and markets for Japan, influences Japan's foreign policy in many ways.

Were it not to contribute to the preservation of their stability, Japan would suffer not only in economic but also in political and strategic terms. The economic and political fate of these countries has a direct connection with the Japanese-US partnership. One major external stimulant to the economic growth of many East Asian countries has been the receptive US market. Growing US protectionism is leading to an increasing number of trade conflicts with these East Asian states and forcing Japan to become a substitute, as far as possible, for the US market. There is also the risk that these growing frictions between the United States and Asia could lead to a reorientation of US-Asian relations, which would in turn affect Japanese-US relations. The US reaction is also closing one route for Japanese indirect exports to the United States, via Japanese subsidiaries in East Asian countries. In short, providing markets to the region is helping Japan's fight against worldwide protectionism as well as enhancing Japanese-US relations.

Japan's backing of the Philippines is motivated less by direct economic interests (which are considerable) than by support for the maintenance of the US military presence in Asia and regional cohesion within ASEAN. Japan has long been conscious of its position as the sole Asian country at the annual Western economic summit meetings. At recent summit meetings Japan has been prominent in bringing the interests of the Asian countries to the attention of the other six powers. It has been active in summit discussions on regional issues such as the Korean peninsula or Indochina, as well as, since 1987, the economic situation facing the NIEs.

Japan has recently been trying to diffuse the problems created by the trade surpluses of the East Asian countries with the West and the limited foreign access to their markets by bringing them into some kind of special dialogue with the OECD. The OECD ministerial meeting in May 1988 endorsed a Japanese initiative, which led to an informal dialogue between representatives of the OECD and the four NIEs in Paris in January 1989. Former Prime Minister Nakasone proposed a sort of Pacific OECD or GATT, but this proposal is still frowned upon by the weaker East Asian states, which fear the emergence of a club for the rich. However, other countries like Australia, South Korea and Thailand seem to be interested in creating a loosely organized forum which would give the Asian-Pacific region more clout in future trade negotiations.

In the 1960s and 1970s Japanese politicians and academics were particularly interested in promoting the idea of a Pacific Economic Community which, although vaguely defined, took some inspiration from the EC. The Japanese economist, Kojima Kiyoshi, gained some attention through his proposal for a free-trade zone among the five industrialized Pacific countries (Japan, the United States, Australia, New Zealand and Canada), and in 1968 Foreign Minister Miki Takeo proposed to the countries concerned the setting up of a Pacific Economic Community. Soon afterwards, however, Japan dropped the proposal because it excluded the other Asian countries. More concrete ideas, aimed at ameliorating contacts and communications between all Pacific rim countries, came out of the Pacific Basin Cooperation Study Group established by Prime Minister Ohira in 1979.

In 1980, Ohira and the Australian Prime Minister, Malcolm Fraser, founded the Pacific Economic Cooperation Conference (PECC), a trilateral body comprising representatives from government, business and academia. The PECC was warmly embraced by Japan, which funds its secretariat through the Japanese Institute of International Affairs, an organization affiliated to the Foreign Ministry. A loosely defined and unofficial group, the PECC has modest aims, attempting to facilitate and promote the exchange of capital, technology, goods, information, academic research and culture. In 1988 a Japanese proposal for a $1 million central fund as a financial base for PECC was agreed. Some interpret this as a first step towards an organization, although there is not yet a central secretariat. Membership issues are no longer as divisive as in the past, and the Soviet Union has been accepted as an observer, with China and Taiwan already as full members. Some Latin American countries have also been granted observer status and it is conceivable that their wish to become full members will eventually be approved.

Regional diversity and the lingering fear amongst Japan's neighbours of being dominated by Japan will certainly prevent a group which would resemble the EC. The ASEAN countries, for example, are ambivalent about Japanese economic power; they welcome aid and investment but are concerned about their heavy trade dependence on Japan; ASEAN's trade total with Japan amounted to $35.1 billion in 1987, compared with $27.5 billion with the United States and $22.2 billion with the EC. A too active Japanese role reminds many in the region of the wartime Greater East Asian Co-prosperity Sphere. Japan's neighbours are also suspicious that the group would be of benefit mainly to the most developed countries in the Pacific rim, namely the United States, Canada, Japan, Australia and New Zealand. It is also questionable to what extent a group of countries without a common culture and civilization can be brought together, on no other basis than, for example, the fact that their intra-regional trade has grown to a level of over 60%, as is the case with the 15 PECC members.

However, even a loose grouping could be a challenge to Europe's role in world trade and its link to the most dynamic region in the world. Since 1981 successive Japanese prime ministers have gone on record as saying that any Pacific grouping should be non-exclusionist. Europe's role will depend also on the nature of Western Europe after 1992. Should Japan, the United States and other Asian countries perceive European integration efforts as protectionist, this might well give more impetus to something like a free-trade zone. Certainly there are those within the region who publicly promote the idea of a free-trade zone in order to influence the development of Europe up to 1992.

But seen from Japan, a regional grouping where Japan would at least be one of the major players must have certain attractions for the Japanese. It would help them to overcome their feeling of isolation, brought about by the country's geographic situation and the lack of horizontal integration in the political and economic systems in East Asia. It would at least loosen Japan's trade dependence on the United States without endangering the security alliance, while giving it more backing in its dealings with the United States. Rising economic and political frictions could only increase the attraction of opting for 'regionalism'.

9
CONCLUSIONS

Japan's position in the world at the end of the 1980s is in many ways on a par with that of the United States and the Soviet Union. But whereas the two superpowers have huge natural advantages in terms of their large populations, physical size and natural resource endowments, the power of Japan's foreign policy is based rather on 'soft' conditions, such as the country's economic performance, its social cohesion and purposefulness, its adaptability to challenges from the outside, its alliance with the United States and its integration into the Western world. Nevertheless, in many of its dimensions Japan's foreign policy is comparable to those of the superpowers because of the global outreach of its influence, based on its superior economic performance which is gradually being translated into political, and even military, power. Japan has become indispensable for the management of the global economic system and the maintenance of international security. For the United States, in particular, Japan has become the most important single country in supporting its superpower status. For most countries in its own East Asian region, Japan is the principal trading partner, investor and provider of aid and technology. For the Third World, Japan is now the biggest single aid donor.

Japan has achieved such an important status within a very short time – over the past decade and a half. It has nevertheless been very reluctant to accept the many consequences of its economic success, be it the opening of its market to trading partners, increased defence efforts or more aid for refugees. Despite the concept of comprehensive security, Japan's reactions to these consequences and outside demands have been rather *ad hoc*. This reactive pattern can easily be criticized, but its flexibility has served Japan very well so far in a rapidly changing world.

Developments in the 1970s and 1980s in the external environment of Japan have led to a shift of emphasis in the concepts of bilateralism, regionalism and globalism which dominate its foreign policy. The bilateralist orientation epitomized by the comprehensive relationship with the United States, with its strong economic and security pillars, is still the most important one. For the foreseeable future it is inconceivable that the United States can be rivalled or replaced by any other country in a bilateral relationship with Japan, or that Japan will adopt a unilateralist approach.

During the 1980s the relationship with the United States has become much closer, and its nature has changed to one of more genuine interdependence and equality, but it is still marred by tensions. The reasons lie in the growing gap in economic power and competitiveness between the two countries and the inadequacy and incompatibility of both socio-political systems in adjusting smoothly to these changes in national power. Whereas the United States tends to urge its allies to take over more international responsibility in order to compensate for the relative decrease in its own economic power, Japan has problems in casting off its perception of being a weak and dependent country and realizing the full impact of its integration into the world economy. At the same time, the United States sometimes fails to understand that more responsibility for Japan in the economic sphere means relatively less US (and European) influence.

Although Japan now has fewer inhibitions about acting on the basis of its economic power in the purely economic sphere, it remains restrained in the area of security. Here greater efforts could actually mean, in the end, less security if its neighbours were to perceive increased Japanese rearmament as a threat, during a period of weakening US control. For this reason successive Japanese cabinets have emphasized that Japan will not become a great military power. During the next few years more American voices will be heard demanding that Japan take over defence responsibilities from the US at a time of major budgetary cuts; finding a new balance of burden-sharing without alarming Japan's neighbours will be crucial. In the last year of the Reagan administration some officials spelled out this concern. Richard L. Armitage, Assistant Secretary of Defense, asked in February 1988, of those demanding more Japanese spending on military forces: 'What would the additional funds be used for? A nuclear capability? Offensive projection forces? Professor [Paul] Kennedy speaks of Japanese carrier task forces and long range missiles – is that what Congress wants? Will that enhance stability in East Asia?'[14] What is not spelled out here is the question of whether a stronger Japanese deterrent can still be controlled and integrated into the bilateral relationship, as is the case today.

The economic relationship will face further hardship as the United States awakens to its budgetary and trade deficits. It can only be hoped that harsh rhetoric and the temptation to use the strengthened Trade Act will not make the United States forget the increasing interdependence of both countries. No longer can either break away from the other without suffering unacceptable damage. Japan will have to further open up its markets, but this alone will not eliminate US economic woes. It is encouraging that representatives of big business in Japan, such as the Keidanren, understand the need for 'even more progress in eliminating residual import restrictions and in simplifying and rationalizing import related procedures'.[15] The risk is that concentration on minor market-opening measures, such as in the very sensitive rice market, or succumbing to the temptation of managed trade with fixed market shares for US business in Japan would create so many frictions that more constructive approaches would become politically submerged.

Europe has become more central to political as well as economic concerns for Japan. The main reasons for this are the prospect of a more unitarian European market after 1992 and the need for increasing trilateral coordination of world affairs. We have seen that 1992 is a challenge for Japanese-European relations as it may lead either to European isolationism and bloc-building (if Europe cannot cope with the industrial challenge), or to the renaissance of a strong Europe in world affairs. Recent indications are that Western Europe and Japan realize the importance of a fruitful, less acrimonious relationship, which looks beyond the issues of trade imbalances and sectoral trade problems. Japan is increasing its investment in Europe, just as it has done in the United States. However, the danger exists that a rather short-term problem (the Japanese trade surplus), which can be manipulated by unilateral and bilateral protectionist measures, is being replaced by a long-term problem of an investment imbalance, which will be much more difficult to solve. It is easier to frustrate the European customer by denying free access to cheaper Japanese products than by eliminating jobs which have been created by Japanese manufacturing investment in Europe. This long-term development must be addressed as early as possible. It is more important than the investment-generated frictions now being recognized by Japanese business leaders as resulting from differences in business practices, problems in corporate-community relations and the over-concentration of certain foreign industries.[16] The 'on-site' Japanese lessons will be lost if Europe does not revitalize its industry and business in order to compete more effectively with Japan. Better vocational and management training will be necessary to facilitate a technology transfer to European industry and to establish an independent, viable and future-orientated high-technology base.

In the security field, the strengthening of Japanese-US military ties and Japan's responsiveness to US demands in the trade sphere demonstrate the power over Japan which the security relationship gives to the United States, although its relative force in global terms is declining. Because of distance and history, there is no way that Western Europe can match this security link by developing similarly close relations with Japan. Japan's foreign and security policies have to take into consideration a power constellation in Asia which is more diffuse than in Europe, where the relationship with the Soviet Union occupies a central place. Moreover, for obvious geographical reasons, Japan is simply more interested than Western Europe in Asia.

In addition, Western Europe, Japan and other US allies in Asia are all competing with one another for a meaningful US contribution to their security. The relative decline of US power and the shift of US economic activities to the Pacific Basin will only intensify this competition, since US forces will increasingly be deployed where American economic interests are most at stake. Japan is less concerned about the risks of US withdrawal than Western Europe. Although the US military presence does cause problems in Japan because of geographical restrictions and overpopulation, a heavy maritime presence in a cooperative environment may, in the long run, be more sustainable than a sizeable deployment of ground forces such as in Western Europe. Whereas Europeans worry about the continued commitment of the United States to their security, the Japanese are concerned that closer racial and cultural ties between the United States and Europe will tilt the balance of attention to Western Europe in times of crisis. Given the volatility of the situation in the Persian Gulf, Japan continues to be worried that the United States may swing forces from East Asia to that region.

The regionalist orientation in Japan's foreign policy has recently been strengthened, even though the original Pacific Economic Community concept had to be buried at the beginning of the 1980s for lack of communality. However, the increase of economic flows amongst the Pacific rim countries and the economic success of its members has led to greater interdependence. Gradually, Japan is taking over the role of the United States as the major market for the products of the region. Japan is investing heavily in Asia in order to offset the steep rise in the value of the yen. The divides between Japan and Asia are evaporating and Japan can no longer regard itself as 'an ultra-modern skyscraper towering alone above a vast garbage dump called Asia', as a well-known Japanese political critic put it in 1986.[17] Japan now feels it has a mission to represent Asia at international economic fora such as the economic summit meetings and the OECD, and is eager to find some formula for a regional grouping which will fare better than the Pacific Economic Community concept.

It is essential for Europe to follow these developments very closely as, relative to the United States, it is disadvantaged in geographical and political terms with regard to the Asian-Pacific region. To make any impact, Europe has to rely almost entirely on an enhancement of its economic weight in the region through the opening of its own market and through joint ventures. Politically it can work through various multilateral economic bodies as well as increasing consultation with the major regional actors, notably Japan.

Japan's new relationship with Asia will depend on how wisely Japan translates its economic preponderance into leadership, on the management of potential instability in several Asian hot-spots such as the Philippines or the Korean peninsula, and on the attitude of the United States. Japan's position in Asia is much too delicate, for historical reasons as well as because of contemporary fears of dominance in the other Asian countries, to allow the emergence of a Japan-led bloc. Moreover, the economic forces behind globalistic policies are much too strong. The willingness and capability of the United States to participate in this Pacific economic integration, to manage its economic friction with Japan and other Asian countries, and to maintain its security commitments in the area will be of crucial importance. The success of the economic and political transformation in China will also deeply affect Japan's relations with Asia. For the time being China needs Japan, but once it is confident of its modernization or changes its modernization policy it may conduct a foreign and security policy which is seen as inimical by several Asian countries and which might bring it into confrontation with Japan.

The globalist orientation has gained strength since the first oil crisis in 1973. It is propelled by the relative decline of the United States and by Japan's advance to economic and financial superpower status. Pushed by the United States and other advanced Western countries to assume more responsibilities for the joint management of the international economy and security, Japan has finally become actively involved in these issues. As with its regionalist policies, however, the need for globalist policies cannot be met without addressing the pressing issues in Japan's relationship with the United States. In many cases globalist policies even demand a strengthening of bilateralism.

A further conclusion from this is that the 'Pax Americana' will not be replaced by a 'Pax Nipponica'. There is no possibility that Japan will replace the United States as a hegemonic power. The size and demographic development of its population, the physical limitations of the Japanese islands, and the size and structure of its economy will not allow Japan to reach the status of a traditional world leader. There is also no political will, supported by sufficient domestic forces, to encourage and sustain such a development. Moreover, as the United States is experiencing now, political and economic interdependence has reached a degree unknown to earlier hegemonic powers. The more Japan expands and prospers economically, the more it becomes dependent on other countries. Japan will have to further open up its economy, which, in turn, will naturally become more vulnerable to the vicissitudes of the total world economy. Japan's rising investment abroad cannot be protected by military power, but only by participation in the management of international politics and economics.

The greatest challenge ahead for Japan's foreign policy will be to respond appropriately to increasing trade conflicts, protectionist tendencies and Third World economic crises. Japan's domestic economic structure has undergone significant changes, but these have so far not had a decisive influence on Japan's trade and investment balance with its major partners. The Japanese will have to learn that the world is unjust: those who work hardest and most efficiently cannot demand that the rewards be distributed accordingly, because over-achievers depend also on those in situations where social rigidity or other unfavourable conditions are hampering necessary restructuring or even leading to decline.

One key question is: do domestic circumstances allow Japan to adjust to these challenges? The survey in Chapter 3 of domestic actors in foreign policy-making showed that the political leadership is rather weak and diffuse and the requirements of the ruling party's pork-barrel politics are very stringent. There is resentment at the ever-increasing demands from the outside to change political and economic approaches. Should the leadership open the country to such an extent that Japan, as many of its people fear, loses its unique identity and culture? It would be very difficult to draw an objective line beyond which Japan's identity would be lost. However, given Japan's international political and economic involvement, there has to be some dilution of traditional approaches. Indeed, Japan has been quite successful in providing new blends of Japanese and foreign management techniques, such as those which have been adopted in various countries hosting Japanese investment. Its rapid economic and political adjustments in the 1980s have proved that Japan has a considerable capability to adjust to the kind of demands, resulting from its very economic success, which would have brought any country with a lesser degree of homogeneity and national purpose to the brink of political or even social disintegration. The question is whether Japan can keep up this responsiveness in the political as well as the economic field, in the face of the growing instability in domestic politics. Neither the United States nor Europe can afford to ignore Japan's answer.

NOTES

1 This conceptual framework has been developed by the author in J.W.M. Chapman, R. Drifte, and I.T.M. Gow (eds), *Japan's Quest for Comprehensive Security: Defence, Diplomacy and Dependence* (Frances Pinter, London, 1983), p. 89ff.

2 *Asahi Shimbun*, 15 September 1988.

3 Comprehensive National Security Study Group, *Report on Comprehensive National Security* (translation, 2 July 1980, Tokyo), pp. 7 and 20.

4 *National Journal*, 30 May 1987, p. 1395.

5 *International Herald Tribune*, 20 July 1978.

6 See Laura Newby, *Sino-Japanese Relations* (Routledge for Royal Institute of International Affairs, London, 1988), pp. 46–7.

7 Bernard Gordon, *Politics and Protectionism in the Pacific*, (Adelphi Paper 228, International Institute for Strategic Studies, London, 1988), pp. 32–7.

8 *International Herald Tribune*, 1 August 1988.

9 *International Herald Tribune*, 28–9 January 1989.

10 *The Financial Times*, 20 June 1988.

11 Report of Defense Science Board Task Force on Defense Semiconductor Dependency, Office of the Under-Secretary of Defense for Acquisition, Washington, February 1987, p. 90.

12 Victor Basiuk, 'Security Recedes', *Foreign Policy*, Winter 1983–4, p. 52; Patricia Schroeder in *International Herald Tribune*, 14 October 1987.

13 *The Financial Times*, 30 June 1988.
14 Richard L. Armitage, 'US Security Role in East Asia', *Defense Issues*, Vol. 3, No. 11.
15 KKC Brief No 51, November 1988 (Keizai Koho Center, Tokyo).
16 Ibid.
17 Hasegawa Keitaro, *Sayonara Ajia*, (Nesco Books, Tokyo, 1986).

Related titles

Sino-Japanese Relations
Laura Newby

The political and economic changes that China and Japan have undergone in the 1980s have not only underlined, but also added to, the complexity of the relationship between these two important East Asian powers. China has seen a key role for Japan in its modernization plans, but has been disappointed by the unbalanced economic partnership formed. Japan has moved towards a higher political profile, but has not found it easy to manage politico-strategic issues with China. The evolution of the relationship in the 1990s – whether towards increasing integration or towards rising tension – will be of crucial importance not only to regional stability and development but also to broader Western interests in East Asia.

Industrial Collaboration with Japan
Louis Turner

This study looks at the experiences of European and American companies that have collaborated with their Japanese competitors in the fields of computers, consumer electronics, automobiles and aero-engines, by forming joint ventures, designing products together, and pursuing complementary marketing strategies. It examines why these companies have chosen to collaborate rather than compete; whether the Japanese have proved to be reliable partners; whether the non-Japanese have been left behind; and what the future of such collaboration may be. The paper concludes by pointing to a growing interest among non-Japanese companies in investing and collaborating within Japan itself.

New from Routledge

Japan at the Summit:
Japan's Role in the Western Alliance and Asian Pacific Cooperation
Shiro Saito

Japan has been under increasing pressure in the 1980s to match its economic involvement in Asia and the West with an equal commitment to international political relations.

Written from a Japanese point of view, this book examines the gradual transformation of Japan's traditional world role since World War II and discusses Japan's recent realization that international cooperation must take place on many diverse levels. Focusing on the Japanese attitude to recent Western summit meetings, the book demonstrates that Japan's sense of political responsibility to other developed nations is now being significantly redefined.

ROUTLEDGE